Communication in Responsible Business

Communication in Responsible Business

Strategies, Concepts, and Cases

Roger N. Conaway and Oliver Laasch

businessexpert
Press

Communication in Responsible Business: Strategies, Concepts, and Cases
Copyright © Business Expert Press, 2012.

First published in 2012 by
Business Expert Press, LLC
222 East 46th Street, New York, NY 10017
www.businessexpertpress.com

ISBN-13: 978-1-60649-324-3 (paperback)

ISBN-13: 978-1-60649-325-0 (e-book)

DOI 10.4128/ 9781606493250

Business Expert Press Corporate Communication collection

Collection ISSN: 2156-8162 (print)
Collection ISSN: 2156-8170 (electronic)

Cover design by Jonathan Pennell
Interior design by Exeter Premedia Services Private Ltd.,
Chennai, India

First edition: 2012

10 9 8 7 6 5 4 3 2 1

Printed in the United States of America.

Abstract

Communication in Responsible Business sets the stage for social, environmental, and ethical business. These topics have risen to the forefront for many businesses and communication of them has become crucial to business success. This book offers an extensive toolbox of the most effective instruments for communicating social, environmental, and ethical business to a variety of stakeholders. Each chapter covers specific situations for communicating responsible business. We provide examples of social and cause-related marketing, sustainability reporting, issues-and crisis communication, the use of vision, mission statements and codes, and web-based stakeholder communication. The book gives practitioners hands-on concepts and actual illustrations. Chapter cases provide rich practical coverage and translate concepts to solutions for day-to-day business realities.

Keywords

Corporate Responsibility, Corporate Sustainability, Business Ethics, Marketing, Communication, Stakeholder Management

Contents

CHAPTER 1

Setting the Stage

CSR principles and the question of how to communicate them represent a challenge for businesses (...), but also an opportunity, as they can potentially increase the financial worth of companies very significantly.[1]

Communicating responsibility is probably the most critical part of the responsible management process. Getting the job right can create value in different ways among the various stakeholders that affect or are affected by your business.[2] Communicating well with these groups is the essence of communicating responsible business.

Let's compare two companies and examine how they communicated social and environmental topics to their stakeholders. One might guess it to be an unequal match between TOMS shoes, a medium-sized shoe company from California and the industry giant Nike, much like a David against Goliath scenario. Surprisingly the smaller company TOMS seems to lead the way in successfully communicating social and environmental business performance.

In 2006, TOMS shoes was founded by the entrepreneur Blake Mycoskie who had no previous experience in the shoe business. The decision about building a shoe company was neither based on special skills nor a perceived business opportunity. TOMS shoes was created from a necessity to help the cause of shoes for poor children in Argentina. After visiting the

Company:	TOMS
Industry:	Shoes
Tool:	Cause-Related Marketing

Lesson: Credibly communicating cause commitment can create immense stakeholder goodwill and, when connected to a product, will serve as a tool to successfully penetrate even mature markets.

(Continued)

(Continued)

country, Mycoskie came up with an idea that at first seemed counter-intuitive. "What about if I started a company and every time I sold a pair of shoes, I gave a pair away?" The "One for One Movement" was born and became the centerpiece around which Mycoskie built his company. Mycoskie's innovative idea was rewarded by almost instant public attention. When the entrepreneur returned to the USA with his first 250 pairs of shoes for kids, newspapers instantly picked up on the story. Immediately following the trip, TOMS sold 22,000 pairs of shoes through its website. By October of 2006 TOMS had sold more than 10,000 pairs of shoes and was ready to give back the same number to poor kids. By October 2010 TOMS had sold and channeled 1,000,000 shoes to children in 23 countries on four continents.[3]

The social and environmental communication tool used by Mycoskie is referred to as cause-related marketing, in which a product's connection to a good cause becomes a sales argument. Cause-related marketing creates a product-anchored commitment and communicates to stakeholders integrity between walk and talk. External media endorsements helped TOMS shoes to become the new rising star in the mature shoe industry.

Another shoe company that is one of the strongest brands worldwide is Nike. Nike has become famous for an ongoing, but so far not very successful, stakeholder dialog about the issue of sweatshop production of its sneakers.

Nike's "sweatshop" issue unfolded in the late 1990s in several episodes, each of which provided profound lessons on how to not communicate social and environmental business performance. By the early 1990s, Nike had developed enormous brand-power, which served as a solid advantage over competitors such as Adidas and Reebok. The secret to Nike's

Company:	Nike
Industry:	Shoes
Tool:	Issues and Crisis Communication

Lesson: The stronger your brand, the more attractive it is to criticism and the weaker the socio-environmental performance of your businesses' core operations, the more vulnerable it is to criticism.

(Continued)

successful business model was based on strong brand recognition achieved by the swoosh logo, "The Just Do It!" slogan, and prestigious sponsor relationships with sports celebrities such as Michael Jordan and Tiger Woods. Another distinct feature of Nike's business performance was the almost complete outsourcing of production activities to low-wage countries, which provided the basis for low operational costs and the possibility of concentrating on its core-competences of marketing and innovation.[4]

It was the very combination of branding and performance that made Nike highly attractive and vulnerable to labor activists' campaigning. On one hand the production operations of Nike left the company open to attack, based on the often questionable labor conditions in provider factories. On the other hand, Nike had much to lose. Damage to Nike's reputation was a considerable threat to the company's competitive advantage. As a matter of fact, during the period of strongest activist criticism, Nike's stock value plunged from $38 per share in 1996 to $19 in mid-1997.[5] While the whole loss cannot necessarily be attributed to the sweatshop criticism, a strong causal connection is likely. The following chapters will highlight interesting aspects of Nike's communicative moves and stakeholders' reactions.

Effective Stakeholder Communication Makes Money Sense!

As shown in the preceding examples, communicating and marketing social and environmental business performance can achieve considerable financial gain or incur significant losses. How positively (or negatively) your various stakeholders perceive your company ultimately translates into financial value creation as seen in the case of TOMS or value destruction as seen for Nike. The mechanisms of value creation differ from one stakeholder to another and from case to case:

- The stakeholder *customer* may react positively with increased willingness to purchase products, such as in the case of TOMS. Or the customer may react negatively with a reduction of consumption of a certain product or even aggressive consumer boycotts. This customer indicator directly influences the amount of revenues generated by the company.

- The stakeholder group of ***investors is*** very sensitive to the future cash flows expected from business operations, as cash flows ultimately translate into dividends. For instance, eco-efficiency reduces operating costs, while investments into sustainable innovation products can open new markets or increase the purchasing price in existing markets. Lower cost and higher revenue jointly result in higher profit margins and higher dividends that will likely be achieved from responsible business activities. Well-managed social, financial, and ethical factors reduce company and investment risk. Risk and profit margin are two decisive factors influencing shareholder goodwill toward the company. Shareholders' rewards are an increase in investment and higher stock prices.

- The ***employee*** stakeholder reacts positively to responsible business conduct in at least three well-documented ways. First, it is easier for a responsible company to attract employees. Studies have revealed tendencies that include a decrease in wage expectations the more responsible a company is considered to be, and a complete refusal to work for a company which is seen as irresponsible. Responsible businesses also often have more contented workers. Work satisfaction increases because of physically improved work conditions and the pride to work for a "good company." Positive financial repercussions range from lower operational costs from higher work efficiency to a reduction in job placement and training costs because of higher employee retention rates.

As illustrated in the preceding three examples, it makes ***money sense*** to keep stakeholders happy by creating goodwill. In order to create stakeholder goodwill, companies have to ***first achieve positive social and environmental performance***, and, ***second, communicate effectively*** the progress made to the stakeholders. Isolated communication activities unconnected to real progress are often labeled as "greenwashing" (see Chapter 2) that may have serious financial consequences.

This book presents suggested management tools for communicating and marketing social and environmental business performance that creates goodwill among the various stakeholder groups connected to any business's activity. Recommended tools vary among stakeholder groups and communication purposes. The social marketing tool, for instance, is used to bring about behavioral change with customers and community stakeholders. Cause-related marketing aims at marketing a product among customer stakeholders and providing a social, environmental, or ethical sales argument such as TOMS does. Reporting tools for responsible business activities primarily are directed at Non-governmental Organizations (NGOs) and investor stakeholders. The following chapters elaborate on powerful *communication tools* for creating stakeholder goodwill among a wide variety of stakeholders. You will also encounter a broad set of real-life business cases that illustrate the application of these tools. A recurrent theme will be topic of congruence between walk and talk, between communication and actual business activity. Communication might appear as attractive and profitable "icing on the cake" (the responsible business); but the most beautiful icing cannot compensate for a distasteful cake. Because of the strong communication focus in this book, we will not provide detailed illustrations of implementation activities. However, we will constantly refer to both implementation flaws and best practices in actual company cases.

Understanding and Communicating Responsible Business

While responsible business in its different versions is a popular buzzword, the term also connotes confusing vagueness. Companies may talk about their sustainability when referring to environmental performance. Additionally, terms like corporate philanthropy and corporate responsibility (CR) are often used as synonyms and social entrepreneurship is often understood as a fashionable new type of NGO. All of the previously mentioned connotations related to responsible business are wrong in a strict sense.

In order to excel in responsible business communication, a *sine-qua-non*, a necessary condition, is needed to clarify what one wants to communicate. Otherwise, misunderstandings will result. Responsible business does not exist in one broadly acknowledged and understood definition, but rather stems from a set of prominent traditions. Each tradition, such as ethics, sustainability, and citizenship, is understood in the context of a broader set of values, practices, terms, and concepts. Once you and your audience have reached a basic understanding in these background areas of responsibility, it becomes easier to decipher meaning, assumptions and the broader contexts behind the words used.

Figure 1.1 illustrates six of the main traditions that have lead to a common understanding of what responsible business is and does. Responsible business conduct in a specific case is always a mixture of characteristics of several of those traditions. For instance, a new Coca Cola PET bottle is designed with up to 30 percent of plant-based plastics and involves the idea of improving the environmental part of the company's **triple bottom line (sustainability).** It also requires a commitment to the customer **stakeholders (responsibility**) and reduces the impact of waste on the **community (citizenship**). Thus, this initiative can be interpreted as a good **ethical decision (ethics**).[6] One could even say that responsible business does not exist as an independent entity, but is a cloud of characteristics borrowed from those background theories.

Attempts to find a generally accepted definition for responsible business or corporate social responsibility (CSR), which has been the current buzzword for the last 20 years, have failed for this very reason. The

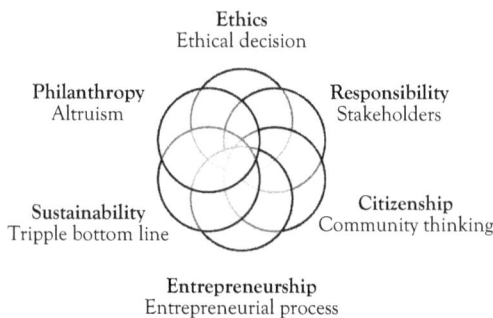

Ethics
Ethical decision

Philanthropy
Altruism

Responsibility
Stakeholders

Sustainability
Tripple bottom line

Citizenship
Community thinking

Entrepreneurship
Entrepreneurial process

Figure 1.1. Responsible business as an intersecting "cloud" of traditions.

mix of characteristics of responsible business is different for every situation, for every company, every business region, every product, and every activity. Through time, several different responsible business background traditions have been accepted as dominant. The 1980s were the time of business ethics. The 1990s to today have been the times of CSR, with a brief interruption highlighting corporate citizenship at the end of the 1990s. It appears that like the second decade of the millennium will be a time of social entrepreneurship.

The following paragraphs illustrate main background traditions, and their respective *core concepts**. Core concepts are important for communication because they are the few "safe areas" that are theoretically sound and generally agreed upon. Understanding these core concepts provides communicators in an emerging field with legitimacy in their own messages and the ability to evaluate or even to question others' usage:

1. Ethics in the form of **business ethics** fosters morally right, **ethical decisions** in business. More than 2000 years of moral philosophy from ancient Greek virtue ethics to late 20th century ethics of rights and justice can be applied in the business context. Communicators who are based in the ethical tradition tend to speak about right, wrong, and morality. They make normative statements about what business should or should not do.

2. Philanthropy in the form of **business philanthropy** centers on the core concept of **altruism.** Business philanthropy can be traced back to early Christian merchants who gave a part of their fortune to the poor and followed the biblical ideal of the Good Samaritan. The word philanthropy has Greek roots and translates as love for mankind. Thus, business philanthropy can be defined as business activities done out of love for mankind. Donations, disaster relief, and volunteering activities often are communicated as philanthropic activities. Communicators based in philanthropic thinking tend to speak about altruism, cover topics with social impact, question businesses' philanthropic motivation, and criticize nonaltruist profit seeking.

---

* The illustrated traditions are presented in a broad chronological order of their emergence.

3. *Business responsibility* involves **stakeholder** perception and the assumption of the responsibilities businesses have to various stakeholder groups. The field of business responsibility began in the early 1950s with the book *Social Responsibility of the Business Man* by Bowen.[7] CSR, CR, corporate social performance, corporate social responsiveness, and business accountability are all related terms. Communicators based in a business-responsibility background typically call for businesses' adoption of responsibility and accountability in relationship with stakeholder groups and critique the idea of shareholders as a business's single principal.

4. Sustainability in the form of *sustainable business* has the so-called *triple bottom* line at its core.[8] The triple bottom line concept integrates social, environmental, and economic outcomes, which are the three pillars to reach sustainable world development. The ultimate goal of the triple bottom line is to assure planetary human survival and wellbeing. The birth of the sustainability tradition goes back to the 1987 Brundtland report of the World Commission for World Development.[9] Communicators based in a sustainability background tend to emphasize intergenerational justice, seek to preserve the planet for the next generations, and focus on "three-dimensional" management style to achieve a sustainable triple bottom line.[10]

5. Citizenship in the form of *business citizenship* has *community thinking* as its core. Companies are seen as citizens of a community and are given the responsibility of contributing to the community's development and wellbeing. Corporate citizenship is the main term of this tradition that held prominence from the mid-1990s to the early 2000s. Community may refer to many types of communities, from the local community a company operates in, to the broad global community. Communicators thinking in citizenship terms will refer to civic responsibilities, social investment and capital, and the political role of companies.

6. Entrepreneurship in the form of *social and environmental entrepreneurship* has at its core the *entrepreneurial process* of seizing opportunities through innovation. Social and environmental entrepreneurs address social and environmental issues with an

entrepreneurial mindset. The actors of entrepreneurial ventures for society and environment might be business founders,[11] entire corporations,[12] or individuals using established organizations as their

Put it to practice!

Learning to "speak the language" of each tradition is an indispensable prerequisite for successfully communicating in responsible business. Check your understanding with the following examples, all quoted exactly from Samsung Electronics 2011 sustainability report.[14]

Mark the respective number (1–6) of the applied background tradition next to each example. Solutions are given in the appendix of the book.

#1 Ethics #2 Philanthropy #3 Responsibility #4 Sustainability #5 Citizenship #6 Entrepreneurship

Statement	Background tradition #
(A) Global harmony with people, society and environment	
(B) Our social contribution endeavors in Africa include an initiative to foster 10,000 local engineers and doing away with illiteracy in the community.[15]	
(C) Currently, the Board of Directors (BOD) is composed of seven members, with four of them being outside directors. The outside directors hold the majority in the BOD, thus ensuring the independence and transparency of the Board's decision-making process.[16]	
(D) We believe that we have a responsibility to resolve social issues while achieving growth. A fast-aging population is a global phenomenon and people are increasingly seeking ways to lead healthy lives. Against this backdrop, Samsung Electronics decided to invest in health care as a future business in 2010 with the objective of improving quality of life and sustaining growth.[17]	
(E) Samsung Electronics is now equipped to log, respond to, and resolve stakeholder queries and concerns in a systematic manner through the development of a global stakeholder communication system.	
(F) Samsung Electronics employees in Korea donated KRW250 million to this cause and the company matched this, raising a total of KRW500 million.[18]	

vehicles.[13] Entrepreneurial approaches became well-known alternatives during the first decade of the new millennium. Communicators applying an entrepreneurial mindset typically refer to social or environmental opportunities, innovative approaches, and social ventures.

However, different these background traditions to responsible business sound in their focus, they have one important characteristic in common. All six traditions result in business activities and performance that go beyond the traditional economic profit imperative and integrate social, environmental, and economic business concerns.

The Myth of Sustainable Business and the Reality of Responsible Business and Management

First of all, there is no such thing as a completely sustainable business. What business could be considered truly sustainable in line with the global sustainable development imperative? A working definition derived from the common understanding of the term will aid in our discussion of sustainability:

> A **sustainable business** (the ultimate goal) is one that has a neutral or even positive environmental footprint, a business that creates positive value for society, and is economically viable or profitable. That is a business with a neutral or positive triple bottom line in all three performance dimensions.

A sustainable business is the proverbial holy grail of responsible business, a myth, but yet to be sought after. Nevertheless, envisioning such a business fulfills an important "lighthouse" function, an imaginary role model for the companies that take responsible business seriously. The wording, sustainable business, which is used by both scholars and practitioners in the field, evokes a wrong impression of businesses that have arrived in their overall sustainable impact. It is more credible to say that sustainable businesses have made a commitment to be responsible businesses and conduct responsible management. In the context of this book, we will frequently use other terms to provide clear understanding Figure 1 illustrates the relationships among these terms.

> A **responsible business** (*committed company*) *is a company that has made a credible commitment and taken action to tackle its **immediate responsibilities** toward a broad set of stakeholders, and progressed toward its **long-term responsibility** to become a sustainable business.*

It is important to emphasize that the term responsible business is not a frequently used term. This infrequent use gives the term the advantage of not having a common meaning or misinterpretations. The definition given above is an umbrella definition, that integrates background traditions from sustainability to ethics. In sum, responsible management refers to management activity that deploys a broad variety of tools for managing social, environmental, and economic business performance:

> **Responsible management** (*the management activity*) is the management activity necessary to achieve the responsible businesses' social, environmental, and economic performance. Responsible management includes planning, implementation, and communication activities.

The responsible management process is based on two types of responsible management instruments. **Specialized responsible management instruments** include stakeholder management, ethics management, and life-cycle impact management (Figure 1.2). Those management instruments

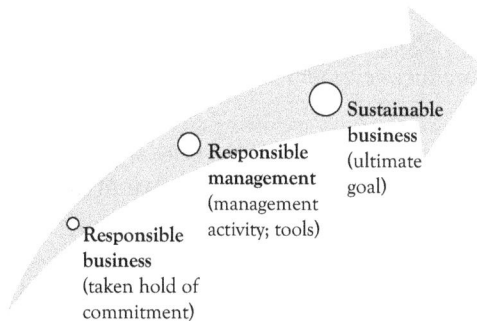

Figure 1.2. Working definitions of central terms.

are cross-functionally important throughout any management activity in responsible business. *Mainstream responsible management instruments* are well-known traditional management instruments that have been adapted to also manage social and environmental business performance. Green logistics, social marketing, sustainability accounting, and sustainable innovation are some examples.[19] Both specific and mainstream responsible management instruments are mostly combined in responsible management activities. Let's apply those working definitions to the two shoe companies illustrated before.

TOMS shoes uses a combination of the **responsible management** *tools as elements of the company's basic business model. The instruments applied are social entrepreneurship, cause-related marketing, and life-cycle assessment. Nike uses sustainable innovation together with sustainable operations management for developing shoes with a lower waste impact. We assume TOMS shoes has made strong commitments to its stakeholders and toward becoming a sustainable business in the long run. We can call this a* **responsible business***. We can also do so for Nike if we assume their commitment to tackle both social responsibilities for third-world employers and to make serious moves toward reducing the environmental footprint of running shoes closer to zero. Until either company has reached a neutral to positive impact in its social, environmental, and economic performance, it cannot be called a* **sustainable business***.*

Our focus in this book is on the communication process of responsible management. As we illustrate in the following section; communication in responsible business is crucial for cross-functional stakeholder management of responsible business activity, from employee volunteering to sustainable product development.

The Role of Communication in Responsible Management

Critics of responsible business communication may doubt the validity of such efforts and call it window-dressing, greenwashing, or a mere public

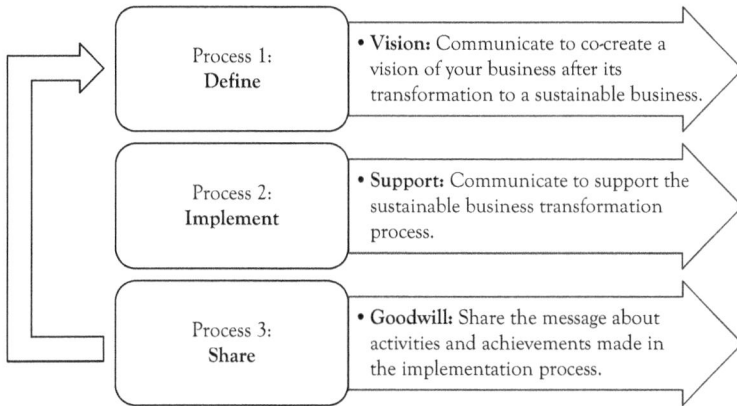

Figure 1.3. Communication processes and their respective goals in sustainable business.

relations exercise. Chapter 2 extensively illustrates how to counter such accusations if they are not justified. In some cases, criticism may be justified due to misunderstanding of the role of communication in responsible business. As Figure 1.3 illustrates, spreading the word about company achievements in the responsibility arena is just one of three functions of responsible business communication[20]:

Responsible business communication helps to **define** what a sustainable business, a sustainable process, and specific stakeholder responsibilities ultimately should look like in an ideal situation. If a business is serious about achieving transformation of stakeholder responsibilities and sustainable business, then drafting a plan must first involve an extensive consultative communication process that includes a broad variety of internal and external stakeholders.

This first process is a crucial prerequisite for communication that helps to **implement** responsible business. During this second process, a company may need to convince key decision makers to support the implementation process and educate stakeholders important to the implementation process. For example, businesses in the implementation stage may use a social marketing campaign to change employees' behavior toward saving energy and water during the production process. Or a business may decide to use cause-marketing communication to create a market for a new sustainable innovation product line.

The third communication process that follows implementation involves *sharing* the message about the business's responsible activities and performance. During this final stage, businesses deploy formal responsibility reports, press releases, advertisements, or other communications to inform stakeholders about both achievements and issues.

Avoid an easy mistake!

The communication goals during these three processes are fundamentally different. During the define phase, the main goal is to co-create a vision of what the business should become, while implementation requires achievement of support for the implementation process. Spreading the word aims at creating goodwill among company stakeholders. Communicators often mix up those functions. A company that seeks to really understand what stakeholders claim and how they integrate into the company's sustainability vision (define) should by no means try to convince stakeholders of how good the company is (share). On the contrary, it may be helpful to involve stakeholders who can identify weaknesses and help co-develop solutions.

Some companies mistakenly start to communicate responsible businesses in reverse sequence from these three processes. Instead of first consciously defining responsible business, then deeply implementing and communicating the results, these companies may choose particular and isolated responsible management activities to actively raise company reputation in a public relations exercise. As illustrated by left-side graph in Figure 1.4, such a reversal may turn out to be a **responsible communication trap,** which at first seems to be an attractive public relations exercise. Stakeholders usually detect such superficial communication efforts. They dig deeper and often uncover outright scandals. In response the company reacts by defending. If stakeholder pressure continues, the company inevitably starts to admit they implemented superficial responsible business activities. In the next step, the company typically realizes the truth that only a long-run, transformative approach to responsible business will appease stakeholders. This chain of events parallels the pattern of events and reactions in the Nike case illustrated at the chapter beginning. Companies can also get trapped by imprudent reporting of

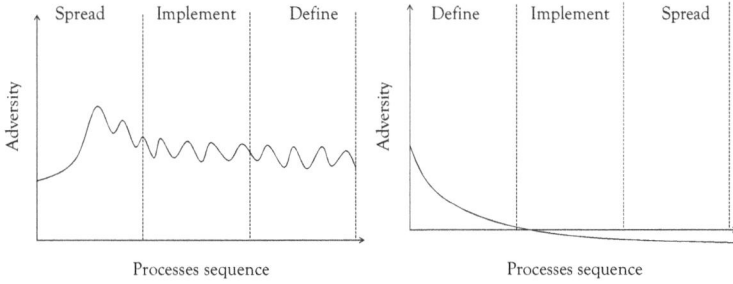

Figure 1.4. Communication trap versus downhill strategy.

communication activities and are forced to implement less than optimal responsible business activities during constant stakeholder adversity.

A positive contrasting mechanism may be called a **down-hill communication strategy** in responsible business (see right graph of Figure 1.4). The down-hill illustration refers to initial adversity that decreases over time. Businesses following the define-implement-share strategy will receive a reputational benefit from stakeholders at a future point in time. When Mycoskie voiced his idea of selling two shoes for the price of one, stakeholders reacted skeptically (define). Skepticism continued when Mycoskie communicated his idea of competing with established US brands. This adversity quickly shifted to positive, active advocacy by stakeholders. Mycoskie received media coverage and speaking events related to the responsible business, which proved to be a main revenue driver at virtually no cost. Active endorsement by customers fascinated by the business also proved to be a revenue driver.[21] The point where adversity becomes advocacy depends on the impression a responsible business makes on stakeholders. This point might not even be reached. Nevertheless, trading a troubled implementation process that has mediocre results for a smooth transformation to responsible business seems to be an attractive deal either way.

Summary

In this chapter we have examined how effective stakeholder communication makes money-sense for business. We have described where responsible business originated and distinguished the different background traditions such as sustainability and ethics. We have also considered how centrally important communication is for responsible business. The next steps depend on you. However, you began your responsible business journey, the key is to see it as exactly this, a journey. The following example used by the NGO, Accountability, in its stakeholder engagement standard, provides a description of this journey:

> *Stakeholder engagement is a journey. The starting point is often pain alleviation. Something bad has happened and there is significant external pressure that needs to be addressed urgently. The organization finds that it needs to engage, to be more transparent, and to respond directly to stakeholder concerns. Organization that find stakeholder engagement has helped resolve a problem, then look for ways to use engagement as a preventive rather than a reactionary mechanism. They begin to use it systematically as part of risk identification and management. They discover that a better understanding of their stakeholders results in an easier and more receptive operating environment. Performance improves. They then discover that it can contribute just as much to strategic as to operational improvement. Engagement can be a tremendous source of innovation and new partnerships. Leading companies are discovering that a growing percentage of innovation is coming from outside the organization and not from within. They realize that stakeholders are a resource and not simply an irritant to be 'managed'. At this level, stakeholder engagement drives strategic direction as well as operational excellence.[22]*

The next chapter provides insight into the topic of greenwashing, a situation where stakeholders perceive that the company is not "walking the talk." This ambiguity evokes a misleading impression of the firm's social and environmental business performance. Greenwashing is probably the most dangerous pitfall for communicators of responsible business.

CHAPTER 2

Walking the Talk: Avoiding Greenwash

(…) the consequences of getting it wrong and being seen as purporting a fraud—or, greenwashing (…) are growing. Whether real or perceived, when consumers see greenwashing, they are likely to punish companies with less sales. When NGOs see it, they are motivated to drive negative campaigns and press. And when regulators see it, they can determine that an environmental claim is a 'deceptive practice' and fine companies.[1]

Businesses would not function and organizations would fail without effective communication, which we define as the process of a message being shared and understood. We all know that communication errors cost businesses in lost productivity, delays in production, broken relationships, and even human lives. Businesses stand to gain economically and increase brand image when CSR communication is effective. Businesses stand to lose when CSR communication breaks down. It is even more important how businesses "walk the talk" in CSR communication and communicate CSR effectively. Greenwashing accusations result when CSR communication is ineffective and results in the "greenwashing trapdoor" for many organizations.

In this chapter we describe how a difference sometimes occurs between what companies *do* and what stakeholders actually *perceive*. Imbalance grows as this difference of perception increases. We also define the concept of "greenwash" and closely relate it to imbalanced communication, but let's first examine Starbuck's communication of its environmental performance.

Starbucks Communication

Few doubt that Starbucks markets successfully its coffee products and communicates effectively about its sustainable brand. The company's website clearly displays a *Responsibility* link in the heading, and the link includes five prominent

Company:	Starbucks
Industry:	Coffee Industry

Lesson: Starbucks illustrates how accurately a company can communicate its sustainability performance (talking the walk) and actually performing what it communicates (walking the talk). The company represents balanced communication.

subcategories of Starbucks' responsibility performance. The Diversity of Suppliers link, for instance, emphasizes the company's priority toward supporting businesses owned by women and racial minorities. The Wellness link lists calories, fat, and sodium content of their beverages and products. This transparency of information communicates well its sustainability performance.

Starbucks responsibility performance also matches its communication content when the accuracy of the company's website is checked by various NGOs. The Ethical Sourcing link, for instance, describes Starbucks Coffee's partnership with Conservation International and Coffee and Farmer Equity (CAFE), an initiative that helps "our farmers grow coffee in a way that's better for both people and the planet."[2] Thus, Starbucks appears to balance marketing of its products and environmental performance with effective communication about that performance. Little difference exists in stakeholders' perception and what Starbucks communicates about CSR activities.

In fact, Starbucks seems to charge higher prices for coffee because of its sustainable brand. According to York[3] in *Advertising Age*, chief marketer Terry Davenport at Starbucks believes pricing decisions are part of the marketing mix. Davenport considers Starbucks coffee not just a product but an idea, in the sense that community and conversation follow around a cup of coffee. The Starbucks idea is how customers enjoy comfortable chairs, free Wi-Fi, and music. Even the specialized coffee vocabulary that Starbucks uses creates a cult-like

(Continued)

following. The company arranges for each store to have unique labels and words for different types of coffee and distinctive flavors of products. Along with the coffee and brand, most customers believe Starbucks is a leader in social and environmental business performance, which enables it to charge higher coffee prices because of its sustainability brand.

Sarah Lozanova,[4] writer for Greenbiz.com, posed the question, "Is Starbucks a leader of sustainability or a greenwasher?" pointing to how the company is both praised and criticized by environmentalists. Although Starbucks has revolutionized the American coffee drinking experience, Lozanova maintains the coffee industry inherently takes its toll on the environment. Each cup of coffee requires 140 liters of water, a high water footprint, but the company has led the coffee industry by reducing its water waste and by decreasing leakage in its dipper wells, which are used to wash utensils. Apparently, the dipper wells previously wasted over 6.2 gallons of water each day. Starbucks also has taken measures to conserve soil and water usage on coffee farms and has made sustainable progress by reducing its water waste and water footprint. Indeed, Starbucks is leading the coffee industry in water conservation and is perceived to be a leader in sustainability.

In what areas can Starbucks improve? Critics identify a lack of recycling infrastructure for customers, and Starbucks agrees. The company has reported that it is on track to develop comprehensive recycling solutions for paper and plastic cups within the next few years. Starbucks reported that it needed improvement in implementing front-of-store recycling in company-owned stores by 2015.[5] Additionally, the company agreed it needed improvement in reaching the goal of serving 25 percent of store beverages in reusable cups by 2015. In 2010 only 1.8 percent of beverages were served in reusable cups. In summary, Starbucks serves as a sustainability leader in the coffee industry and makes continuous progress in responsible areas and, more importantly, the company effectively communicates to stakeholders its progress and areas where it is improving.

Effective Communication Principles and Greenwashing

In this section we describe principles of good communication and the concept of "greenwashing." Following these sound communication principles must be the goal of each person who communicates sustainability messages. We also discuss the crucial CSR activities of effective marketing and communication in a business. Finally, we discuss ways to avoid the greenwash "trapdoor" through balanced communication.

Guiding Principles for Good Communication in Responsible Business

Five guiding communication principles are applicable to social and environmental business performance messages:

1. *Adapt* to the company's stakeholder audience.
2. *Provide transparency* with messages.
3. *Be complete* with information.
4. *Assure accuracy* in everything that is said.
5. *Build goodwill* with stakeholders.

The first communication principle, *adapting to the audience,* implies the company spokesperson asking the following questions: "What questions are stakeholders asking?" "In what are they interested?" Adapting implies the speaker's message addresses topics *important* to the audience and uses words and language at the *level* of the listener. British Petroleum's (BP) initial response to the 2010 oil spill in the Gulf of Mexico did the opposite. It seemed to center on company actions and responses rather than audience questions or interests. Most people listening to the news, from business owners along the coast line to environmentalists, were concerned about the impact of the spill on their businesses and lifestyles, not on BP's safety record, environmental policies, or the company's planned responses to the crisis.

In addition to the lack of audience adaptation, BP's messages also lacked *transparency.* The initial public messages seemed to give the impression BP was hiding something. Additionally, information about the amount of oil in the water was *incomplete* and *inaccurate.* The number of barrels of oil spewing from the broken pipeline was grossly underestimated, and the spread of the oil in the water turned out to be in a much greater volume than first reported by BP. The company's communications did everything but build goodwill with stakeholders. BP's messages missed developing a positive tone and relational style toward stakeholders. Much more could be said about these principles, but the central idea is that effective stakeholder communication involves all five of these basic principles. When applied to CSR messages, these principles will improve a firm's communication, avoid greenwash accusations, maintain reputations, and strengthen economic bottom lines.

Effective Marketing and Communication

Effective marketing and communication in a business are crucial CSR activities. The messages that stakeholders and the public receive about CSR determine what they perceive about economic, social, and environmental business performance. CSR messages may be sent through many channels, including traditional television or advertising media, web-based messages, or new media. We stress in this chapter how *balanced* communication must be the goal of these messages in whatever channel is used. Imbalance occurs when a business is sustainable, in that it creates value in numerous social or environmental activities, but the communication is weak in that it does not say much about those activities to customers, employees, and other stakeholders. When this lack of information happens, the company is indeed making progress toward becoming a sustainable company, but it has ineffectively communicated that message. Another extreme imbalance can occur when a business does not engage in many sustainable activities, but creates the impression that it does. The business may create the impression through marketing and communication that it has a good sustainable performance when not much actually exists. Creating these false impressions may be intended to gain favor with customers or promote a product. Intense marketing and communication occurs, but in reality the company creates little social or environmental value for stakeholders. Communication and marketing must match the company's sustainable performance, and when that balance exists the business is "walking the talk" and "talking the walk."

The Greenwashing Trapdoor

What is greenwashing anyway? While many uses of the term "greenwashing" exist we will refer to it "as marketing and communication activities that are designed to create a misleading impression of a company's socio-environmental stakeholder value creation." Greenwashing occurs when a company miscommunicates messages that exaggerate its actual socio-environmental performance. Effective marketing communication must match the business' actual performance of creating stakeholder value. Thus balanced communication means the company is "walking the talk" and "talking the walk." The Foresight Sustainable Business Alliance (FSBA), a proactive business group near Chicago, IL, USA, frequently checks business communication about sustainability. The FSBA characterizes greenwashing as disinformation that misleads the public. A company that communicates its environmental performance with unsubstantiated or irrelevant claims is open to greenwashing accusations.[6]

Refer to Figure 2.1 to better understand the greenwashing trapdoor. Note that the four-pane window represents (1) a horizontal continuum of low to high social and environmental performance, which we will call stakeholder value creation, and (2) a vertical continuum of low- to high-communication effectiveness about that performance. Start at the left side of the window and move horizontally to the right. The left point on the horizontal continuum represents low amounts and low intensity of communication about the sustainable activity. As you move to the right, the amount and intensity of communication increases. Now, start again at the lower, bottom left point of the window and move directly upward. This vertical dimension represents the degree of value created for stakeholders. Low value created would position a company at the bottom of the dimension while high value created for stakeholders would position the company near the top of the dimension. In essence four window panes are created based on (1) low value, low communication, (2) high value, low communication, (3) low value, high communication, and (4) high value, high communication.

Thus we label the top left box "shy" because it represents the company that engages in significant sustainable activities but doesn't communicate well about those activities. Performance is strong but communication is

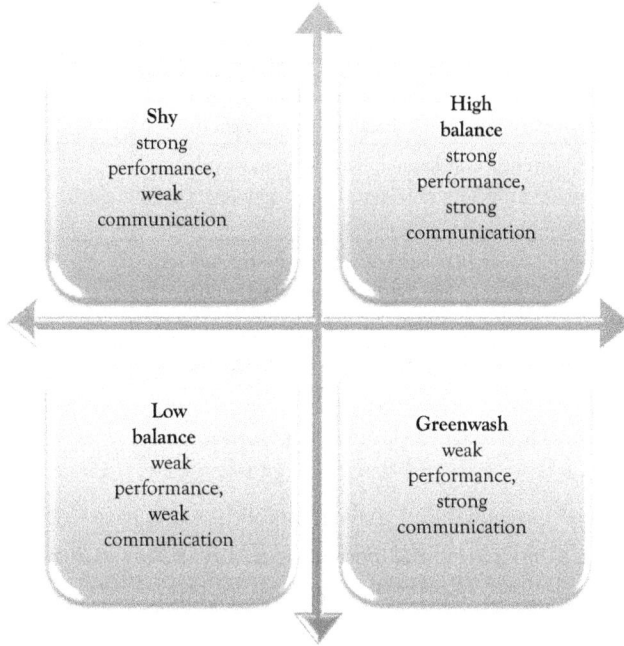

Figure 2.1. Stakeholder value/effective communication.

Sources: Adapted from Horiuchi, Schuchard, Shea, & Townsend (2009) and Taubken & Leibold (2010).

weak and many stakeholders are not aware of the performance. On the other hand the lower right box represents a different approach. The company's performance is weak but strong communication gives the impression of a strong performance. The company is open to greenwashing accusations in this case. Companies want to move to the High Balance position of strong performance and strong communication of sustainable activities. Let's example various Starbuck's sustainable activities according this four-pane window.

Put it to Practice!

Using Starbucks as an example, match the four primary dimensions of stakeholder value and effective communication we discussed in Figure 2.1. Write either (1) **low balance**, (2) **shy**, (3) **greenwash**, or (4) **high balance** in the appropriate space on the right.

Dimension	Communication balance
Starbucks takes decisive action to reduce water leakage in its dipper wells but few people know about the company efforts.	
Starbucks actively engages stakeholders in dialog about reducing water usage and as a result exceeds it sustainable performance goals for the year.	
Critics identify how Starbucks lacks recycling infrastructure for customers and Starbucks agrees, but the company takes no action to develop recycling solutions.	
Starbucks reports how it significantly reduces disposable cups in its stores but its actual performance fell below its stated goals.	

Answers: 1= shy, 2= high balance, 3= low balance, 4= greenwash.

We suggest sustainability goals be established that have "high balance" in social and environmental performance and strong communication. The company "walks the talk" by doing what it communicates, but it also "talks the walk" by communicating about what it is doing. Remember this "window" of stakeholder value and effective communication is from the perspective of the business. Sometimes stakeholder perceptions differ from company perceptions. Let's examine "shy" communication from Italian-based LensCrafters optical shops.

LensCrafters Communication

LensCrafters illustrates a "shy" business because it creates value in social performance but does not effectively communicate those sustainable activities. The optical retail chain, located in Canada, the U.S., and Puerto Rico, is considered North America's largest seller of eyewear and

Company: LensCrafters

Industry: Visual Health Industry

Lesson: LensCrafters illustrates a "shy" company that is performing notable social activities but communicates little about what those activities. Shy companies can benefit greatly by communicating effectively those activities.

related services based on sales. The company of 14,000 employees has 955 stores and is owned by Italy's Luxottica Group SpA.[7] Luxottica owns the Ray-Ban and Oakley brands and the company reported that

(Continued)

"its net profit in 2011 rose 13% to €456 million ($613.9 million) on sales up 7.3% to €6.223 billion."[8] It was "the very first optical retailer to promise eyeglasses in about an hour."[9] The stores offer a full range of vision services, including independent doctors of optometry, laboratories, and prescription frames and sunglasses by Luxottica. LensCrafters represents a large company involved in significant social performance, but one that communicates little about those social activities on its own web page.

The LensCrafters social foundation called OneSight, started in 1988 and is related directly to its core business of helping customers with their vision needs. The OneSight foundation purposes to "give someone else the gift of sight," especially the poor who can least afford corrective lens and eyewear. LensCrafters stores collect used eye glasses donated by customers and send the eyewear internationally to global clinics. The foundation has operations all around the world. In many African countries a large truck with LensCrafters painted on the side can be seen taking doctors and equipment to remote places. OneSight identifies itself as "a family of vision care programs dedicated to restoring and preserving clear vision to those in need through outreach, research and education, in order to hand-deliver the gift of sight to those in need worldwide."[10]

Despite the size of the company and the significance of the One-Sight foundation, little information is communicated publicly on the LensCrafters main website. The foundation has existed for over 20 years. Information about OneSight is difficult to find through the LensCrafters website, although the foundation has its own URL at www.OneSight.org. No visible links are available on the main page. While information about the social activity may benefit the company, LensCrafters seems to communicate about it only indirectly with the public. We can only speculate at this strategy, but perhaps the company fears investors will criticize the program as a misappropriation of company funds. In contrast, significant data exist that show most investors seek companies that demonstrate sustainable performance, and LensCrafters promotion of OneSight would most likely influence positively investors' decisions. Thus, the economic bottom line may benefit from stronger communication.

(Continued)

(*Continued*)

Another reason for lack of strong communication about the foundation may be that LensCrafters believes customers will perceive their brand negatively because company resources are directed toward social activities. However, most buyers today chose to purchase products from a business involved in sustainable activities over one not involved in sustainable performance, when the product's price is about the same. All things being equal, effective communication from LensCrafters about its environmental or social performance would enhance the company's bottom line, reputation, brand image, and customer loyalty.

Ethics

We have discussed sound principles of communication, CSR marketing, and how to avoid the greenwash trapdoor. Let's turn now to CSR marketing, communication, and ethics. We will examine the close connection between communication and marketing ethics. We will also briefly introduce integrated marketing communication (IMC) and illustrate how Johnson & Johnson exemplifies CSR marketing communication.

Communication and Marketing Ethics

Viewing marketing and communication as an integrated concept, termed officially in marketing as *Integrated Marketing Communication (IMC)*, implies that all communication from an organization should interconnect into a single, unified message directed toward building stakeholder goodwill. This integration of marketing and communication applies both internally and externally. Sometimes organizations may unintentionally communicate different messages to stakeholders or may duplicate the same message unnecessarily in different departments. An advertising department may emphasize the stylish design of a newly offered product, while the sales department focuses on customer service of a different core product. The marketing department may convey yet a different message about growth in sustainability performance of products. All of these messages may be important within the company's strategy, yet customers become confused with the different emphases.

When messages are integrated in all areas of internal and external communication, communication effectiveness occurs and it helps to avoid unnecessary duplication and possible conflict of information.

The newest American Marketing Association (AMA) definition of marketing, generally accepted in Europe and North America, reflects market orientation rather than company orientation. The association's current definition of marketing includes a component of social responsibility and value for consumers in society at large: "Marketing is the activity, set of institutions, and processes for creating, communicating, delivering, and exchanging offerings that have value for customers, clients, partners, and society at large."[11] Similarly, the United Nations Environment Programme[12] has stated, "From marketing to advertising, from corporate communication to public awareness campaigns, the messages of sustainability are embodied in practices that are increasingly well-established." Thus, a company's communication about product, price, place or distribution of products, and promotion must be increasing embedded with messages about sustainability performance. Next, consider how Johnson & Johnson communicates sustainability about one of its most popular products, the popular Band-Aid brand adhesive.

Johnson & Johnson's IMC

The popular Band-Aid brand adhesive has been a favorite among parents who sooth the scrape on their child's elbow with the loving touch of a band aid. The Band-Aid

Company:	Johnson & Johnson's
Industry:	Personal Care
Lesson: Johnson & Johnson illustrates how design and green issues interconnect for successful branding and sales.	

brand is synonymous with a parent's love. To keep the product popular, Johnson & Johnson redesigned the Band-Aid brand box to maintain its popularity but with a sustainable strategy in mind. Most of all, Johnson & Johnson has communicated effectively about the new changes. *Advertising Age* recognized the company's new innovations in 2006. Johnson & Johnson was rated as one of the best 10 innovative marketers that year.[13]

(Continued)

(*Continued*)

Chris Hacker, senior VP-global design and design strategy at Johnson & Johnson, tells the story of innovation in the Band-Aid box and how eco-sustainability can be achieved through design. He said, "it's not only easy being green, it's been easy to bring green to one of the biggest playing fields in consumer products" at Johnson & Johnson.[14] One such achievement stands out. Through Hacker's leadership, the company developed a new, environmentally friendly box design for the popular Band-Aid brand adhesive. He started with "packaging-weight reduction and the use of recyclable and certified materials; biodegradability and reusability are the next step."[15] Before the new innovation, the Band-Aid packaging came from Brazil from unknown source material. Now, the new packaging materials are made from Forest Stewardship Council (FSC)-certified paper by a Brazilian facility that produces about 90 percent of the boxes from trees in responsibly managed forests.

Johnson & Johnson's messages about innovation illustrate well the integration of marketing, communication, and responsible management. The Band-Aid brand box remains as popular as ever, and its environmental footprint has been greatly reduced, an illustration of effective communication and marketing at Johnson & Johnson.

IMC in CSR

Richard Weaver[16] once wrote that our language is inherently "sermonic," implying that values and ethics are intrinsic to all human language. Consider for a moment all the choices you make when putting together a message about a CSR activity. It's not possible to include all information about the activity. You must make choices about which important points should be included. This selection process reflects what is valuable to you or the company, and involves attitudes, choices, character, or standards of conduct. CSR messages comprise explicitly stated or implied value statements about the sustainable activity, such as "how the good work of our foundation benefited the poor," reflecting the value that helping the poor is good. In essence, language attempts to shape the perceptions of stakeholders in ways that attempt to persuade, influence, or motivate them to accept our view of the world. In any message, ethical principles and values merge with sustainability through marketing and communication.

According to the Ethics Resource Center,[17] values are those "core beliefs we hold regarding what is right and fair in terms of our actions and our interactions with others." Values involve what is worthwhile and of importance to us. When we communicate our marketing decisions, those decisions are based on those values and our ethics come into play. Thus, ethical decision making by a company involves key choices that mirror company values and marketing messages involves ethics.

Using External Endorsements

In the following section we will examine two important ways a company uses external endorsements in marketing and communication: through eco-labeling and positioning itself as a top-green company.

Eco-labeling

Let's examine one growing area of marketing today. How does eco-labeling accurately reflect sustainability of a product and packaging? In early 2012 the ecolabelindex.com website was tracking over 420 eco-labels in 246 countries and 25 industries. The significance of effective eco-labeling will continue to grow and it will help promote confidence in consumers that the sustainability of the product is accurate. The FSC stands out as an excellent example. It is an independent, nongovernmental organization that promotes responsible forest management worldwide. Begun in 1993 as a response to concerns over global deforestation, the Council began to promote responsible management of the world's forests. The FSC emblem is often seen in a wide variety of products. Some academic textbooks even certify that paper used in the book was from a responsibly managed forest. When a significant eco-label such as the FSC appears on packaging, customers know that the product they have purchased with the FSC label means the entire supply chain of the product was monitored for sustainability.

Ethical choices are involved in each labeling decision, packaging decision, or decision to choose the type of package coloring when marketing products. Decision makers must ask, how accurate is the label? Does the green colored leaf or emblem on our product accurately represent product sustainability? Or will it slightly mislead the customer? Dinah Koehler and Chris Park[18] reported an extensive survey by Deloitte of senior sustainability executives in large multinational companies. They reported that Deloitte interviewed the executives to understand motivations behind eco-labeling. Four distinct eco-labeling strategic decisions appeared to emerge:

- Companies want to maintain market share in areas with mandated green purchasing guidelines. The labels enabled the company to maintain and increase market share.
- Companies use the eco-label to increase their chances of winning large institutional contracts. In other words, the eco-label helped purchasing agents to have a clear indication of sustainable performance.
- Companies believed eco-labels raised the visibility of their sustainability initiatives and strengthened their long term competitive advantage.
- Companies use eco-labels for "brand play" where the eco-label aligns with the brand strategy. For whatever reasons companies place eco-labels on its products, an eco-label may not increase value if brand value is already high, but in most cases the label will enhance value.

So what are ethical reasons for using eco-labels? Each of these four executive strategic decisions is based on value judgments and ethical choices related to sustainability, and all are made based upon the company's strategy. The fourth strategy, for example, involves "brand play," a situation where the decision-maker adopts an eco-label to enhance the value of a brand. Thus, if the eco-label decision involves "puffing" or exaggeration, the decision inaccurately reflects the sustainable nature of the product and the marketing misrepresents the product's impact on the environment.

Top Green Companies

Consider the larger area of green branding of products by large companies and the marketing involved. Large international businesses can build ethical, sustainable brands. But the largest companies in the world are not always known as the greenest companies. Table 2.1 displays Newsweek's often cited list of the top 10 global green brands. According to Forbes,[19] Newsweek's methodology "focused on each company's environmental footprint, environmental-related management policies and the company's disclosure and reporting practices." Each company then received a total score in the three categories that determined the final rankings. Interestingly, the company's communication through disclosure and reporting practices was an important criterion in the ranking. Social activities were not included in the evaluation, only environmental.

Table 2.1. Newsweek World's Greenest Companies

1. Munich Re	6. BT Group
2. IBM	7. Tata Consultancy Services
3. National Australia Bank	8. Infosys
4. Bradesco	9. Philips Elec
5. ANZ Banking Group	10. Swisscom

Source: Forbes (2011).

Munich Re, a large German-based reinsurance company that markets the slogan "Thinking further: How will we Live Tomorrow?" topped the list of the world's greenest companies. IBM ranked second because it "conserved more than 5.4 billion kilowatt hours of electricity, saving $400 million, between 1990 and 2010."[20] Effective communication fused with ethical practices about sustainable activities, such as transparency in disclosure and accuracy in reporting practices, helped these brands reach the top 10 green companies of Newsweek's list.

A marketing and ethics issue arose recently concerning McDonald's Happy Meal products.[21] We will discuss this case again in detail in Chapter 4, but in May 2011 approximately 550 health professionals pressured McDonald's to stop marketing Happy Meals because of the junk-food risks to children. The coalition of professionals cited the health epidemic of obesity in children and asked that McDonald's retire Ronald McDonald by ending the marketing campaign. The professionals published the letter as full-page ads in six large city newspapers around the U.S. to leverage their influence with the company. In an effort to do what was right with children, McDonald's responded by improving the nutrition (reducing calories and fat) of Happy Meals sold in North and South America and included fruit and smaller portions of fries with the meals. The company was not acting illegally by marketing Happy Meals to kids, but ethical issues clearly were involved.

McDonald's communication to its stakeholders illustrates ethical standards of disclosure, transparency, and accurate reporting of information. According to Mark Gunther,[22] the company is moving to mainstream sustainability by making changes that include "LED lights in new and renovated stores. 'Greener' packaging. Eco-labels on fish sold in Europe." Gunther reported that Bob Langert, vice president of sustainability, seeks to embed sustainability in all operations and eventually into the McDonald's brand. Yet many critics still believe the company must make greater efforts at transparency and disclosure. In the end, we agree McDonald's communication is "sermonic" in that it reflects values and ethics of the company. Yet the corporate messages to the public often focus on the best, persuasive aspects of its sustainable activities.

Summary

In this chapter we began by examining effective communication principles and greenwashing. We established a foundation of five communication principles intrinsic to effective CSR communication. We offer these principles as a standard, rubric, or type of scorecard, for *ethical practices* in CSR communication. We suggest you set a goal of constructing messages that (1) *adapt* to the company's stakeholder audience, are (2) *transparency*, (3) *complete* with information, (4) *accurate* in what is said, and (5) *build goodwill* with stakeholders. To totally achieve these five communication principles in each message is difficult, but it is indeed a goal.

Beginning with sound communication principles, we next discussed *balanced* CSR communication, which implies communication and marketing must match or identify accurately the company's sustainable performance. High balance exists when the business is "walking the talk" and "talking the walk." When imbalance occurs, "greenwashing" accusations from stakeholders are more likely to occur. We referred to greenwashing "as marketing and communication activities that are designed to create a misleading impression of a company's socio-environmental stakeholder value creation." Balanced communication helps the company avoid the greenwashing trapdoor.

We also viewed marketing and communication as an integrated concept, IMC, and urged companies to ensure all organizational messages interconnect into a single, unified message directed toward building stakeholder goodwill. The importance of guaranteeing that internal and external messages integrate together cannot be understated. This integration allows communication effectiveness to occur and helps to avoid unnecessary duplication and possible conflict of information.

The second major section covered communication and marketing ethics. We believe values and ethics are intrinsic to all human language, in whatever context, time, or culture. Each message we make involves ethical choices to shape stakeholder perceptions. These choices underlie what the company values and promotes through communication and marketing about its sustainability performance.

In the final section, we looked at how companies use external endorsements of eco-labeling and "green" branding. Eco-labeling represents a growing area of marketing today. We also saw how large international businesses can build ethical, sustainable brands.

CHAPTER 3

Stakeholder Communication: Integrated and Strategic

Notably, the spirit of CSR pervades every aspect of ... business: the corporate mission, production and packaging, human resources management and importantly, marketing, including its communication strategy.[1]

Imagine you are the marketing manager incharge of creating a market for an advanced sustainable innovation product. Assume it's a revolutionary new fair trade coffee. The product is structured in a way that completely reinvests all profits into developing communities of small coffee farmers around the world. Assume further the strategic intent behind this activity is to be an attention-getter. It will signal the company's commitment to fair trade and will create a strategic product differentiation that allows for placing a wide variety of for-profit fair trade products in the newly opened market segment. So far so good. Much money is spent, the product is placed, and media attention is overwhelming. However, in the course of the hype, a lower level employee is asked by a media source for an opinion on the new product. The answer "I am very happy for those poor farmers, but why don't they take care of us employees first?" The comment triggers an endless stream of negative attention about your company's employment practices, revealing extensive shortcomings. The overall result: The new product launch fails as the company loses the credibility for fair trade, and the company's reputation is seriously damaged. Employees further lose motivation in their overall performance.

How can good intentions go so awry? This fictional example (which is not far from truth for some companies) can teach us two important lessons.

First of all, communication in responsible business serves impressive strategic advantages when aligned with overall business **strategy** and tactics. Second, **integration** of communication throughout the company is key for successfully communicating in responsible business. All communication channels must be integrated into a consistent message. External and internal communication must be clear and coherent, and messages must be in congruence with company reality and core business. Thus, integrated communication reaches all important stakeholder groups of a business.

In the following examples we will consider CEMEX, the world's largest building-material corporation and Deutsche Bank (DB), one of the world's largest commercial banks. CEMEX has championed integration of communication, and DB has shown impressive practices in applying communication for strategic purposes.

The Mexico-based global leader in construction materials, CEMEX, has been able to integrate its message of social responsibility through a wide variety of communication channels. In reviewing the company's main themes in responsible business, it becomes clear how well-defined and aligned the company's message is. CEMEX's signature topic in responsible business is com-

Company: CEMEX

Industry: Construction materials

Tool: Integrated stakeholder communication

Lesson: Integration of communication tools and the message sent internally and externally to a broad set of stakeholders, provides a coherent picture, crucial for achieving credibility.

munity impact. The main program "Patrimonio Hoy" is a business model that provides poor people with their own home, and it aligns closely with CEMEX's core business. The program has been covered as a role-model example in many books and business school cases,[2] resulting in no cost, high-impact positive communication. CEMEX's company slogan is "building the future" (construyendo el futuro) which aligns with the title of the company's responsible business report "building a better future."[3] Unlike most other businesses, CEMEX prepares not only one but ten global report versions to reach local stakeholders in their own languages (English, Spanish,

(Continued)

German, French, Polish, etc.). The global report is available in the online "investors center," while local language reports are linked to country home-pages. CEMEX also communicates to its suppliers, a strategic stakeholder group, and through an internet platform in cooperation with the World Bank and the Monterrey Institute for Technology. Suppliers can participate in a 50-hour e-learning course designed by the company to improve sup-pliers' social performance.[4] Recurrent themes are building community and sustainable development (related to infrastructure development).

Next, DB has shown impressive evidence throughout the years in actively using both strategic stakeholder communication and communication of responsible business activities that helps the bank achieve tactical and strategic advantages. The following description covers two important activities.

*Deutsche Bank (DB) is head-quartered in an impressive twin-towered skyscraper in the German finance metropolis of Frankfurt. The two towers com-monly referred to as "Debit and Credit" have in recent years received an additional nick-name, "**the Greentowers**," referring to extensive renovation efforts to comply with the high-*

Company: Deutsche Bank

Industry: Finance

Tool: Strategic stakeholder communication

Lesson: Stakeholder communica-tion tactics can support the creation of tangible benefits from responsi-ble business communication and strategic advantages.

est Leadership in Energy and Environmental Design (LEED) sustainable building standards. The location could not have been chosen better for tac-tical communication purposes. While DB rarely caters to the average pri-vate international customer, they do so in Germany, where these customers are the most critical local stakeholders for DB. The potential for reputa-tional gains from locating in the Greentowers is high in Germany because of a long environmentalist tradition: the average German customer is very sensitive to environmental topics. The Greentowers are located right in

(Continued)

(*Continued*)

*the middle of a transportation hub of Europe's second most active airport,
numerous railway tracks, water transportation on the river Main, and
four main highways surrounding the Frankfurt city center. The 155 meters
high Greentowers are located visibly in the middle of the transportation
hub. This central location constantly communicates a message of exemplary
environmental performance.*[5]

*DB even managed to build a competitive advantage from strategic
stakeholder communication during the subprime crisis. The bank's most
prominent tactical move aroused the anger of the German government
when DB's chief executive officer Ackermann stated that the company
would never accept any governmental aid, let alone a rescue package.*[6]
*The move was superficially seen as less than clever. Yet, analyzing it from
a tactical stakeholder communication perspective, it becomes clear how
beneficial the decision was for DB's strategic stance. The governmental fury
created unique media and stakeholder attention, allowing DB to communicate its message of being the strongest and safest bank in the industry.
Spreading this reputational message was worth arousing the anger of the
government. As one of DB's stakeholders, the government had an urgent
need to get the rescue package accepted, but it had neither the power nor
legitimacy to influence DB's behavior in this case. Meanwhile, strategic
stakeholders such as customers, business partners, and employees were not
fully approving of Mr. Ackermann's message, but they understood the picture of DB being an outstandingly solid enterprise, which is a priceless
attribute in the banking sector where trust is a crucial asset.*

Basics of Stakeholder Management and Communication

Stakeholder communication is foundational for stakeholder management. In this context, we will consider three central **tools of stakeholder
management**: stakeholder mapping, materiality assessment, and stakeholder segmentation. In this instance, stakeholders refer to all groups and
individuals that have a relationship with the company. Stakeholders typically included in a business' **stakeholder map** are employees, customers,
suppliers, communities, governments, NGOs, and owners of the business. The term shareholder is often confused with the term stakeholder.

Shareholders are owners of the business and have a very clearly defined relationship with the company. Therefore, they are one specific type of stakeholder. Competitors are the most frequently forgotten stakeholder because of their often antagonistic relationship. Competitors, however, also have the potential to enter into cooperation and jointly create responsible business solutions on an industry or market level. An exemplary Stakeholder map is illustrated in Figure 3.1.

After an organization has mapped its most important stakeholders, the second step is to understand those stakeholders' claims and balance them with company's necessities. Claims are related to social, environmental, and ethical **issues** in the realm of a certain business. Assessment of so-called issues or materiality **assessment involves a** simultaneous review of the importance and impact of issues to both stakeholders and the business.[7]

Figure 3. 2 illustrates a materiality assessment of four general issues that might be encountered in many businesses. The **materiality chart** analyses the issues for DB and CEMEX. For instance, the issue of employee ethics (e.g., irresponsible sales and investment practices) in the banking business is a topic broadly criticized by stakeholders. Bad employee ethics and neglect of fiduciary responsibilities in banking can cause enormous direct financial and reputational damage in a business where trust is key. Accordingly, the overall materiality of employee ethics is high in the banking business. For CEMEX on the other hand, employee ethics is of only intermediate materiality and importance to both stakeholders and

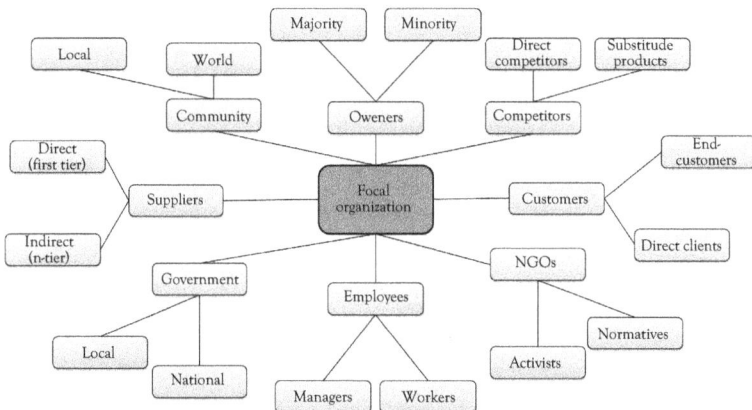

Figure 3.1. Mapping typical stakeholders.

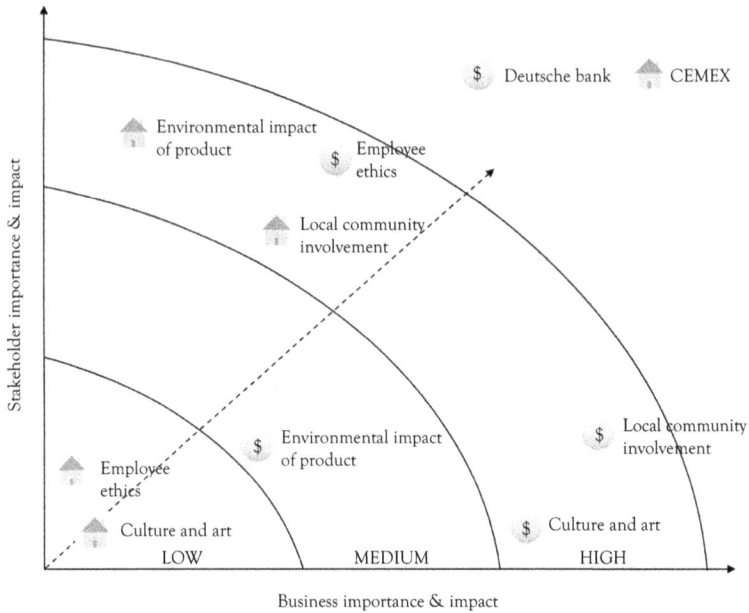

Figure 3.2. Comparing DB's and CEMEX' materiality in selected issues.

the business. The issue of community involvement is of high materiality to both companies, but for different reasons. Traditionally, communities have looked to CEMEX for donations in many kinds of public construction projects, from parks to kindergartens. For CEMEX stakeholders, the company's local community involvement is salient and almost natural. The company in recent year has made community involvement an important part of its business model, which increases its importance.

Deutsche Bank practices community involvement in two main activities, volunteering and microfinance. Both are important parts of DB's business model. Volunteering brings manifold advantages for human resources and microfinance is a lucrative new branch of banking business. In the general stakeholder perception, banking businesses are not necessarily involved in the community beyond representation by branches. Materiality assessments are an important basis identifying priorities in both implementation of solutions and communication. The assessments are also a necessary requirement for reporting responsible business, according to Global Reporting Initiative (GRI) guidelines, which will be further illustrated in Chapter 6.

Materiality assessment serves to identify common interests in stakeholders groups and identifies segments of similar stakeholders. Other exemplary characteristics for stakeholder segmentation might be their attitude toward the company (from antagonistic to supportive), potential for cooperation, legitimacy, urgency, and power of stakeholders.[8] Segmentation is a practice traditionally applied in marketing management, which brings important advantages to messages in responsible business communication. Clearly defined stakeholder segments help to reduce complexity and are crucial to stakeholder management and indispensable for stakeholder communication. Segments help to shape the message, identify communication channels, recognize potential communication barriers, and set the tone of the message.

Put it to Practice!

Imagining you work for DB and have the task of creating a communication plan to heighten awareness about the new Greentowers. Identify into which segments you would allocate the following three stakeholders:

1. **German private customers** are highly sensitive to environmental topics and often display critical attitudes, which require well-implemented plans and effective communication of responsible business activities.
2. **Employees of DB** are highly professionalized and often internationalized. DB is often perceived as one of the best employers in the German banking business.
3. **Green building certification organizations**, such as the US American LEED organization are able to increase the credibility of greening projects by a highly rigorous and widely trusted certification process.
4. **The antibanking movement Occupy** are camping a short distance away from the bank's Greentowers in the Taunusanlage park. The movement focuses on the social consequences of banking practices. The Frankfurt group has proven to be one of the most important worldwide locations for the movement.

(Continued)

(*Continued*)

5. **Joshka Fisher** is a former 1970s radical, socialist-environmental activist, who first turned one of the most influential members of the German Green Party in the 1990. He later became German foreign affairs minister and vice-chancellor of Germany. In 2007 he opened up Joshka Fischer Consulting, focusing on environmental topics, which has recently worked with the German multinational BMW.[9]

The groups and individuals mentioned might potentially belong into one or several of the groups.

...Segment	Characteristic	Segment incumbents
(A) Supporters	Have the potential and willingness to strengthen and stabilize the company's responsible business activities and communication efforts.	
(B) Catalysts	Have the potential and willingness to boost the company's responsible business activities and communication efforts.	
(C) Saboteurs	Have highly critical attitude toward the company or the activity and are likely to hinder implementation and communication.	
(D) Collaborators	Formally participate in the responsible business activity and/or in related communication activities.	

How to Talk with Stakeholders: Communication Tools and Modes

Two prerequisites for successful stakeholder communication include clearly defining the tools which will be used to reach stakeholders and the manner in which those tools are applied. The **communication mode** can be divided into three categories, differing in communication focus and intensity.[10]

1. The **stakeholder information** strategy. In this effort, responsible business communicators communicate favorable social and

environmental business performance in a one-way communication, aimed at creating goodwill among stakeholders who are
important for company reputation.

2. The **stakeholder response** strategy. Communicators choose to react
   to concrete stakeholder concerns, requests or tendencies. The goal of
   such a strategy is to appease critical stakeholders or to use positive
   requests to support information strategies.

3. **The stakeholder involvement** strategy. Responsible business communication requires the most effort with this strategy. Stakeholders
   are engaged into an intensive two-way dialog on an equal level. The
   communication goal is to translate stakeholder input into concrete
   actions and to co-create solutions.

What similarities do the tool of issues and crisis communication
(ICC) have in common with web-based communication (WBC) in
responsible business? At first glance, you may not note significant similarities. While the defining element of ICC is its usage with critical topics, WBC is defined by the use of internet technology. While one tool is
based on issue quality, the other is based on a specific communication
channel; the internet. Both are indispensable elements of communicating
in responsible business.

*Communication tools for responsible management are the unique
mixture of messages, modes, procedures, frameworks which have
the common purpose of communicating social, environmental, and
economic topics to a wide set of business stakeholders.*

Table 3.1 provides an overview of important communication tools
in responsible businesses that are covered in this book. Taken together,
these instruments provide a versatile, highlyeffective toolbox for communication needs encountered in responsible business. Each of the
instruments summarized in the table are illustrated in depth in the following chapters.

Table 3.1. Characteristics of Communication Tools

Tool/chapter	Description	Examples	Mode/process	Stakeholder
Issues and crisis communication (Chapter 4)	Communicating that involves critical topics, such as issues faced by companies or the mitigation of a current social, environmental or ethical crisis.	Ford Motor Co., Maple Leaf Foods, Domino's Pizza, British Petroleum, Toys "R" Us, Apple	Response/spread	Investors, employees, customers
Institutional documents (Chapter 5)	Vision, mission, and values statements, codes of ethics and conduct.	BMW, Procter & Gamble, Toyota, Pepsi, Coca Cola, Cengage, Walmart	Information/ implement	Employees, suppliers, investors
Reporting (Chapter 6)	Establishment of formal reports of single activities or overall company performance, neutral in style and tone, often based on the Global Reporting Initiative (GRI) guidelines.	SEKEM, Itaúsa Brazil, Clorox, Munich Airport	Information/ spread	Investors, varied
Social marketing (Chapter 7)	Usage of traditional marketing management methodologies to achieve a change in behavior, beneficial for society or environment.	Starbucks, Innocent Smoothies, Glaxo Smith Kline, TOMS shoes, Volkswagen	Response/ implement	Customers, employees, general public
Cause-related marketing (Chapter 7)	Usage of social or environmental causes for either increasing sales of a product or brand-power.	American Express, McDonald's, RED	Involvement/ implement + spread	Customers
Nonverbal communication (Chapter8)	Usage of design and structure of structures, processes, products and services as "intrinsic-passive" communicators of responsible business.	Toyota, Innocent Smoothies, Lego, Pepsico, British Petroleum	Response/spread	Varied
Web-based communication (Chapter 9)	Usage of web-based tools such as traditional websites, blogs, social networks, simulations, e-meeting and e-learning tools.	Google, Timberland, Nike+Apple, BBVA, The Guardian	Involvement/ define	Varied

How to Integrate Communication

IMC has become a buzzword. Even the American Marketing Association's definition of marketing exceeds the traditional understanding of marketing as the process of selling to customers. It reads *"Marketing is the activity, set of institutions, and processes for creating, communicating, delivering, and exchanging offerings that have value for customers, clients, partners, and society at large."*[11]

IMC has developed from a narrow initial effort to integrating all communication channels to send a consistent message about products and services Subsequently, the definition of marketing has been broadened to including the effects of communication on brand value. The most recent and broadest understanding describes IMC as a means for "purposeful" exchange to create and maintain "profitable" relationships with any kind of stakeholder.[12] Customers are only one out of many stakeholders in the current understanding of IMC. Marketing is seen as relationship marketing rather than product marketing, which is stakeholder communication in its purest sense. Table 3.2 exemplifies how the company Samsung Electronics manages its integrated communication with various stakeholder groups.[13]

Table 3.2. Integrated Stakeholder Communication at Samsung

Stake-holder	Communication activities	Major issues in 2010
Customers	Customer satisfaction surveys by outside agencies, "prosumer" initiatives, response to CSR inquiries	- Timely launch of new products, enhanced product safety - Increased CSR support for partner companies, ban on conflict minerals from Africa
Business partners	Family Satisfaction Index, onsite interview, collaboration meetings, exchange meetings, best practice workshops	- Ensuring stable supply, rational pricing decisions - Mutual growth programs
Shareholders/investors	One-on-one meetings	- Pursuit of new growth businesses - Risk management
NGOs	Press conferences, response to CSR-related inquiries	- Ban on conflict minerals from Africa - Employee health and safety

(Continued)

Employees	Employee satisfaction surveys, labor council, grievance procedure system	- Work-life balance, creative organizational culture - Worker diversity
Local communities	Local community conferences, volunteer service centers	- Social contribution activities - Partnership with local communities
Government	Conferences, councils, workshops	- Addressing climate change - Mutual growth programs
Press	Forums, news coverage support, press conferences	- Employee health and safety, new growth businesses - Integrity management

Integrated stakeholder communication as applied in this book goes beyond mere integration of the company's communication channels. It includes all the following elements to be integrated that achieve the highest qualitative level in integrated stakeholder communication.

1. **Communication channels**: All external and internal communication channels must send the same message content, which is aligned with a concise set of communication goals following the company's overall strategy.
2. **Stakeholders groups**: All stakeholders must receive a consistent overall message. This message will be similar, but not identical. Different stakeholders require customization of the message due to their segment's different characteristics.
3. **Departments**: For communicators to achieve 1 and 2, it is crucial to coordinate communication within the departments of marketing, public relations, and human resources (main stakeholder communicators).
4. **Walk and talk**: Messages sent must reflect the business' social, environmental, and economic performance. Integrating what a business does and communicates is crucial to establishing credibility. The walk-talk ratio needs to be balanced, always tending toward more walk than talk.
5. **Goal structure**: Aspired outcomes of stakeholder communication must be balanced between company and stakeholder benefit. Otherwise, stakeholders might react negatively or even sabotage outcomes that are perceived as egoistically benefitting the communicating company.

If these five points are followed, integration is likely to lead to integrity and contradiction free, wholesome, and credible communication.

Instrumental Communication: Tactical, Aligned and Strategic

The term "strategy" in common usage is often understood as "any action that has been planned to achieve a certain advantage." The business context requires a more specific usage, which is why we will use the term "instrumental" when referring to the common understanding. In Chapter 1 we considered how creating goodwill among stakeholders may lead to a variety of advantages from motivated employees to increased sales. In this section you will be given insight into the process of instrumentally achieving these advantages. Instrumental communication can serve the good of both the company and of the issue addressed with a specific responsible business activity.

The goal of instrumental communication is to create a mutually reinforcing strategy for improving company competitiveness and mitigates the issue addressed.[14] Communication can be instrumental, actively pursuing a company advantage, in three different ways, which will be illustrated in the following paragraphs. Three **instrumental communication approaches** are shown in Figure 3.3:

Aligned communication in responsible business, aims at creating synergies between primary company characteristics and communication activities. **DB,** for example, focuses as one of its main responsible business

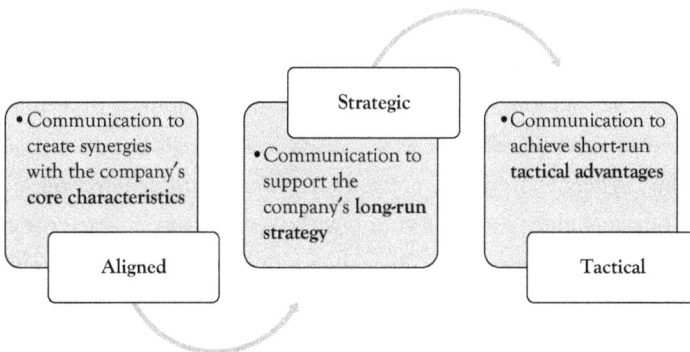

- Communication to create synergies with the company's **core characteristics**

  Aligned

- Strategic
- Communication to support the company's **long-run strategy**

- Communication to achieve short-run **tactical advantages**

  Tactical

Figure 3.3. Instrumental communication approaches.

causes and communication activities on microfinance. This theme of their communication is perfectly aligned with the company's strong reputation of being a banking business at the international forefront of expertise. **CEMEX** does the same thing by using a recurrent theme centered on the word "building," an excellent choice for a construction business. The building theme trickles down from its company slogan to many lower tier communication activities in responsible business. "Building the future" for instance translates into building homes for low-income stakeholders and building infrastructure.[15]

For a food business such as Danone, a similar slogan sounds rather clumsy. The dairy products company **Danone** used the slogan "we build their dreams" (construyamos sus sueños) as a broadly communicated title for the company's cause-related marketing campaign helping children with cancer. **Campbell Soup** on the other hand, is able to connect the responsibility message well to the company's core business. Their slogan is "nurturing the planet." The world's third biggest movie theater chain **Cinépolis** interestingly connected the core business theme (seeing movies) to their signature responsible business activity that gives back eyesight to people with cataracts. Critical stakeholders, however, may question the expertise of a movie business to organize a medical campaign that conducts 3000 surgeries a year.[16] Walmart displayed another form of alignment in their bold move toward corn-based renewable plastics for packaging. **Walmart** has a reputation of being the no frills low-cost discounter and may have encountered an adverse effect if it had tried to communicate a new costly philanthropy activity. The change in packaging probably has saved Walmart economically when oil prices rose and the price of oil-based plastic wrapping increased. This change goes well with what stakeholders would have expected of a company "with Walmart's reputation." The positive environmental impact of Walmart's decision was considerable.[17]

Thus, synergies are always created when a company achieves the alignment of stakeholder communication with the company characteristics of core-business **expertise** (e.g., DB), **theme** (e.g., Cinépolis), and **reputation** (e.g., Walmart). A responsible business communication measure will gain credibility and potency when aligned with company characteristics, and the specific characteristics are also enhanced. For instance, CEMEX communicated messages aligned with construction for the poor and the company will receive valuable feedback to improve its expertise.

Strategic communication in responsible business refers to communication processes that support the company's overall strategy. Company strategy usually is subdivided into three hierarchical levels, corporate level strategy, strategic business unit level, and functional level. The highest level is **corporate level strategy**, which aims at defining a perfect mix of markets and businesses as elements of the corporation.

The CLOROX Corporation, known for its flagship bleach product, decided to include into their business portfolio two high-profile responsible businesses. The company communicated that they wanted to learn how to "green their operations" from the acquired natural products company Burt's Bees.[18] CLOROX also created the responsible business Greenworks from scratch, which produces more environmental-friendly cleaning products as an alternative to the company's more harmful product portfolio. Those moves by Clorox were successful. However, a similar story went awry when L'Oreal, which had been under constant attack from antianimal testing activists, acquired the environmental enterprise The Body Shop and failed to clearly communicate motivation and plans for the business. Feelings ran high and customers even boycotted The Body Shop.[19] CLOROX's corporate level strategy was enhanced by effective stakeholder communication, while L'Oreal's strategy was weakened.

The **strategic business unit level**, also called market level of strategy, applies when companies decide how to compete inside a given market. Two positioning strategies inside a market are either price or differentiation positioning.[20] CEMEX's famous "Patrimonio Hoy" program, for instance, helped to obtain a highly attractive new market. The new position is based on the differentiation of a construction alternative for poor people.[21] Walmart's supplier sustainability code is an example of a company using stakeholder communication to support their price-based market position. The supplier code on one hand improves social- and environmental performance and on the other hand, it also serves as an instrument to collaborate with suppliers, as one of the main cost controlling factors for Walmart.[22]

Functional level strategy, aims at using company departments (functions) to support the company's overall strategy. Stakeholder communication can be an important facilitator to increase single functions contribution overall strategy. Cause-related marketing, for instance, has proven to be a valuable tool for the marketing function. Stakeholder communication with employees is crucial for human resources.

Tactical communication aims at achieving short run, directly tangible advantages. In the DB introductory anecdote, we saw how the DB CEO enraged one not-so-strategic stakeholder in order to get his message of a stable bank through to the other, strategic stakeholders. Tactical communication needs to be used with caution. A tactic that might look very profitable today may change its value quickly. Stakeholders that are not important today may become a major player in the future. Tactical communication in responsible business should only be used when aligned with the company's overall strategy, which provides a long-run perspective.

Summary

This chapter has equipped you with the basics of stakeholder management, including how to establish a stakeholder map and how to conduct a materiality assessment. You have also learned about important stakeholder-communication tools and methods and how to connect those methods to an integrated communication, which goes beyond traditional silo thinking. You have also been provided tools for instrumental stakeholder communication, which creates a mutually reinforcing relationship with your organization's strategy and to harnesses the communication process to achieve tactical advantages for the best of both your company and the good cause.

The following chapter provides guidance on how to use stakeholder communication to steer your company through times of hardship. Issues and crisis communication is the tool that provides you with the necessary skills to successfully confront social and environmental issues, and to overcome crises related to business responsibility or irresponsibility.

Put It to Practice!

Use the following checklist to plan or assess your company's stakeholder communication practice based on the frameworks proposed in this chapter.

Task	Assessment
(A) Assess stakeholders: My company has applied the main instruments of stakeholder management as a basis for subsequent communication measures. Specifically, my company has established (1) a stakeholder map (2) materiality assessment, and (3) stakeholder segmentation.	
(B) Communication plan: My company has chosen stakeholder communication mode and tools for each communication measure and summarized the process in a communication plan.	
(C) Integration: My company has planned the implementation of concrete measures to integrate communication in the aspects of (1) channels (2) stakeholder groups (3) departments (4) walk and talk, and (5) goals.	
(D) Instrumentalization: My company has planned to use stakeholder communication as an instrument to achieve concrete benefits. The instrumentalization plan sums up main benefits to achieved in relationship to (1) alignment (2) strategy, and (3) tactics.	

CHAPTER 4

Issues and Crisis Communication: Expecting the Unexpected

Almost every day, in the newspaper, on TV, or over the Web, we follow the plight of organizations in crisis – where something has publicly gone wrong and the world is watching ... we think – "thank goodness, that's not my company"[1]

If someone asked you to identify "major business crises" during the last few years, you would likely have no trouble thinking of one. It seems environmental, social, or financial crises appear almost daily in the headlines and run the gamut of possibilities. The 2011 Japanese earthquake, tsunami, and resulting radioactive release disrupted electronics and automobile supply chains in Asia and the world. Global heath crises and food epidemics have occurred, accidents involving mine cave-ins, hazardous chemicals spills, and Ponzi schemes involving theft of billions of dollars from investors still make today's headlines, and each instance illustrates positive and negative ways to communicate corporate social responsibility.

When a significant crisis impacts a business, the stock price may fall, income sources may dry up, and operating expenses may become too exorbitant for business-as-usual to continue. Each crisis, whether social or environmental, disrupts normal business, tarnishes reputations, negatively affects brand image, and lowers trust with stakeholders. In the year 2000 Ford Motor Co. and Firestone made headlines concerning auto accidents due to faulty tires. The social issue of public safety had made the news and both Firestone and Ford communicated poorly, though differently, about the recall. Firestone denied the problem, and neither company could agree on how to initially announce the crisis. Eventually, the reputations and brands of both companies were tarnished.

The Institute for Crisis Management defines *crisis* as a *significant business disruption that stimulates extensive news media coverage. The resulting public scrutiny will affect the organization's normal operations and also could have a political, legal, financial, and governmental impact on its business.*[2] That is, the news goes public and multiple stakeholders are involved, with a resulting negative impact on company operations, cash flow, reputation, and brand image.

During June 2011, an outbreak of ***Escherichia coli* bacteria** in cucumbers spread among European countries. A social crisis emerged as the source was traced to either Germany or Spain, and each country blamed the other. Angry farmers and growers in Spain dumped their fruits and vegetables outside the Germany consulate, creating a political issue. Sales of Spanish produce to supermarkets across Europe ground to a halt, and fruit and vegetable exporters lost millions of dollars each week. While the sources of the bacteria were eventually determined, this example illustrates how quickly a multiple business crisis can occur, resulting in halted operations, lost money, and bad relations with local government.

Has your business been impacted recently by a social or environmental crisis? Were you personally affected by the crisis, either directly or indirectly? If so, how did your company communicate to stakeholders in response? Perhaps your individual job or position was impacted by the crisis. If effective communication occurred and your company communicated well, perhaps your business reputation was preserved and your response to the crisis turned out positively. If the crisis took its toll on you and your company, perhaps you are looking for answers and ways to better communicate when the next crisis occurs. In this chapter we will provide guidelines for helping you weather the next storm and prepare for the potential impact of a business crisis.

In 2008 Maple Leaf Foods, a major Canadian food processing company, confirmed with the Canadian Food Inspection Agency that listeriosis had been found in their Sure Slice brand roast beef and corned beef products. Although a national health alert was broadcast immediately, 20 people died as a result of the outbreak and over 200 became

Company: Maple Leaf Foods
Industry: Food and Beverage
Tool: Crisis Communication

Lesson: An immediate communication response to a crisis can make the difference as to whether the company survives. Maple Leaf Foods' response was recognized by the Canadian media.

seriously ill. Class action lawsuits were filed that included 5000 complainants. The financial losses to the company ultimately exceeded $50 million.

The listeriosis outbreak was significant in terms of financial loss and potential damage to the company's market value. Yet the CEO's quick, positive communication response using social media was also significant and helped preserve Maple Leaf's reputation and business. "In contrast to organizations that have confronted crisis situations by avoiding and displacing blame, or keeping silent and maintaining a low profile, Maple Leaf opted for a strategy of high visibility."[3]

Immediately following the death of the first victim, Maple Leaf Food's President and CEO Michael Cain recorded a television message in his office that was broadcast on major media and later appeared widely on YouTube. His message was simple, addressing several topics. First, he confirmed that listeria had been found in some of Maple Leaf's products, a necessary admission of the crisis. Next, he explained in simple terms the nature of the listeria bacteria. He did not use complicated medical language or words that were unfamiliar to the general public. His tone was sympathetic, and he expressed deep concern for what had happened. Then he apologized to the families and individuals of those who had lost loved ones and who had otherwise been affected. Finally, he said Maple Leaf was assuming full responsibility for the situation. He did not try to place blame on government policy or regulation.

(*Continued*)

(*Continued*)

The apologetic communication strategy and acceptance of responsibility by Mr. McCain was risky. Yet it was successful. The message
helped restore consumer trust and confidence. He received acclaim
in the major media for the way he handled the crisis and recognition
from the Canadian Press as the top business newsmaker of 2008.

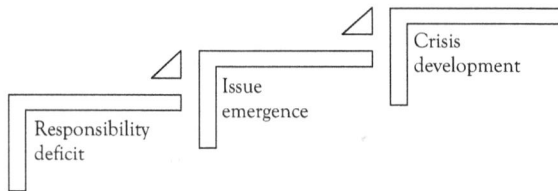

Figure 4.1. The development path of responsibility, issues, and crises.

Basics of Communicating Critical Topics: Issues and Crises

We approach issues and crisis communication through two important
venues. One is internal to the organization and the other external.

Figure 4.1 illustrates how business responsibility, issues, crises, ethics, and CSR are intertwined. The figure shows how crises begin with
a responsibility deficit in the company. The deficit may be a potentially
dangerous workplace condition or labor issue with employees, a potential product liability problem, or an international supply chain process in
manufacturing that suddenly develops into a crisis. If the deficits are not
addressed responsibly, the issues emerge and a crisis develops.

The Importance of External and Internal Issues and Crisis Communication

Communicating critical business topics primarily aims at containing the
negative consequences and harmful stakeholder reactions to such topics. Shareholders might sell their stock, consumers might boycott, and
employees might lose work motivation. As those stakeholders are located
inside and outside the company, effective issues and crisis communication

must use both external and internal venues. Both venues are illustrated in the Maple Leaf foods case. The company's effective *internal communication*, which lies at the core of strong business productivity and occurs as part of the organization's plan of operation, accelerated into action as the crisis occurred. Face-to-face discussions took place, and phone calls, written messages, and emails were sent internally before President and CEO Michael McCain went public with his crisis response. *Formal* internal communication usually follows authority lines illustrated in the company's organizational chart (downward, upward, and horizontal communication).

We want to stress at this point that effective issues and crisis communication must begin internally with upper management in the boardroom.[4] That is, top personnel can originate internal communication and make it a priority. Because sustainability issues involve every department in a company, communication about these issues requires coordination and synchronization from top management. The Economist Intelligence Unit[5] estimated that by 2012, 30 percent of board level meeting time would be devoted to social and environmental topics related to business performance.

Once Maple Leaf Foods' response was determined internally, Mr. McCain spoke on television and *communicated externally* with different stakeholder groups. He chose to use traditional media in the form of a TV broadcast and not immediately use other external channels such as the company's website and social media including Twitter, Facebook, and blogs. Mr. McCain's crisis response proved to be exemplary and acclaimed.

Effective external communication with stakeholders follows intensive internal communication. External communication is critical with NGOs or activists when the company first establishes policy related to CSR. Palazzo[6] relates the example of ABB, a Swiss-based global engineering company that manufactures electrical power products in over 100 countries and is known for its robotics manufacturing. Sustainability principles are integrated throughout its mission and vision statements, and the company's specific goals and objectives relate to environmental and corporate responsibility.

In 2001 ABB initiated its first social policy by involving stakeholders from 38 countries. Before policy was even established, the network of stakeholders worked together with ABB to launch an environmental management program. The group also created sound reporting procedures for sustainability. ABB exemplifies a dialogue-based approach with stakeholders marked by external communication that was intense and ongoing. The resulting impact engendered goodwill and positive reputation. We will discuss specific avenues of external communication later in the chapter.

How Do Issues and Crises Relate to CSR?

Most company crises begin in social, environmental, or ethical issues and therefore clearly fall into the realm of responsible management. Nike's crisis began after the company was accused of accepting child labor in their suppliers' factories. British Petroleum's (BP) 2010 crisis began after an oil well experienced a blow-out in the Gulf of Mexico and resulted in loss of life and extensive environmental damage. We define issues and crisis communication as that communication which occurs in any situation threatening the reputation of the company.

Crises, ethics, and CSR are indeed intertwined. The Ethics Resource Center (ERC), founded in 1922, is considered to be the U.S.'s oldest nonprofit organization "devoted to the advancement of high ethical standards and practices in public and private institutions."[7] The ERC posts a free report for Corporate Boards and Senior Executives on how to address crises. Interestingly, the report asserts that a crisis is fundamentally about ethics, stating that "People will want to know if you lived up to your values." A crisis event is a test of character witnessed by a global audience. Other companies will observe how you respond and will listen intently to your stakeholder messages. They will note how well you communicate about the crisis and what actions you take, especially if their company is in the same industry as yours.

Issues Communication

First, let's consider the concept of issues communication. The ERC report states "the Company response to crisis—in terms of the standards and values that guide decision-making—can be thoughtfully considered before calamity strikes." By addressing issues strategically before a crisis occurs, a firm may be prepared for the crisis event. In fact, a company can be better positioned at the end of a crisis than at the beginning. Thus, our point is that the ERC reminds us of two types of business crises. The first type is the one we introduced earlier in the chapter – an external public event which is unanticipated, significantly disrupting normal operations and receiving extensive media coverage. The second type is the one that exists before the actual crisis occurs, that "long smoldering, cumulative kind that has its roots in ongoing neglect, carelessness, or procrastination."[8] Such a situation is called an issue and is illustrated in the following McDonald's case.

Recently, McDonald's came under pressure to fire Ronald.[9] In May 2011, more than 550 health professionals and organizations signed a letter to the company asking it to stop marketing junk food to kids and retire Ronald McDonald. The letter, run in the form of full-page ads in six metropolitan newspapers around the U.S., acknowledged that "the contributors to today's (health) epidemic are manifold and a broad societal response is required. But marketing can no longer be ignored as a significant part of this massive problem."[10] One must assume that McDonalds, like most companies, would have thoroughly assessed various social issues, challenges, and threats that could affect their competitive environment. McDonald's apparently did so but chose not to withdraw its Happy Meals. A good strategic plan will identify these specific types of social issues but a company must communicate well in response.

Company: McDonalds

Industry: Food and Beverage

Tool: Issues Communication

Lesson: As a global company McDonald's must engage with stakeholders in sustainability issues. The company eventually changed the contents and marketing of the Happy Meal.

Carroll and Buchholtz[11] identify the slow, developing second type of crisis as *issues management*, the process of anticipating challenges, trends, or events that may mature or evolve into a crisis and substantially affect the firm's stakeholders. Business planners must anticipate and intervene in "any trend, event, controversy, or public policy development that might affect the corporation" (p. 194). Polaroid, for instance, missed the mega shift from film processing to use of all digital cameras, and the company went into bankruptcy. Thus, issues management should occur within the company's strategic planning process and follow its SWOT analysis – an assessment of the firm's strengths, weaknesses, opportunities, and threats. Issues are analyzed within this context. Companies address the second type of crisis when they examine industry competition or conduct an analysis in the external competitor environment.

Timothy Coombs has written extensively about crisis communication and produced a handbook that we recommend, *The Handbook of Crisis Communication*,[12] as a detailed guide for crisis communication. Dr. Coombs describes the online issue threats, particularly how viral contagion on the internet can affect a business' prioritization of issues.[13] He offers issue managers a tool he calls "altering the likelihood" that helps in prioritizing issues and assessing the probability of an issue gaining strength and requiring action.

A viral campaign can spread quickly and become contagious in the public sphere. For example, one campaign began with Amsterdam-based Greenpeace against Switzerland-based Nestlé Company for use of palm oil in its Kit Kat products. The viral spread illustrates how effectively communication through social media can affect the manufacturing of a product. Greenpeace posted on the company's Facebook page that Nestlé imported palm oil from suppliers who were destroying Indonesian rainforests and endangering orangutans. As a result hundreds of environmentally conscious visitors began adding rancorous posts, some even defacing Nestlé's logo and reposting it. Communication through texting and email moves exceedingly quickly.

Two examples illustrate how *issues* in the external environment can become a crisis for companies. The first one concerns the recall of baby bibs by Toys "R" Us, Inc., the second largest supplier of toys in the U.S. behind Walmart. CBS News reported in February 2009 that Toys "R" Us recalled

Company: Toys "R" Us
Industry: Children's Toys
Tool: Issues Communication
Lesson: The reputation of a top supplier of children's toys was tarnished because of a weakness in the supply chain. The company must engage in intensive communication with stakeholders in the future to rebuild its reputation.

(Continued)

160,000 of its vinyl baby bibs because high lead levels found in two bibs made in China had exceeded Toys "R" Us standards. The supplier of the bibs, Hamco, Inc., accounted for nearly 90 percent of all Toys "R" Us bibs. In the end it turned out the bibs were okay, but the reputation of Toys "R" Us had been tarnished, and the children's toy company was widely seen as not caring about the health of children.

Toys "R" Us was criticized for the methods it used to communicate with the public. The only channel of public communication was an 800 number published in major media, where customers could call with questions or ask for additional information. However, most mothers with young children were not in touch with traditional television or newspaper and did not know about the 800 number. Instead, they searched for answers on the web and company website. Toys "R" Us did not post information via their website or blogs, which left many mothers without information and increased the frustration with the company.

Toys "R" Us could have improved its communication with the public via the internet. The company missed a good opportunity to save on confusion and bolster its reputation, and it was a hard lesson. But the issue of problematic international imports had loomed on the horizon for some time. Effective internal communication about the issue may not have prevented the crisis, but it may have helped with preparing a crisis communication plan (CCP) when the crisis occurred.

A second example of an issue developing into a crisis can be seen in the case of Apple, Inc. being charged with poor working conditions at one of its manufacturing plants in Chengdu, China.[14] An explosion occurred on May 20, 2011 in the Hon Hai Precision Industry plant, which manufactures the iPad

Company:	Apple, Inc.
Industry:	Electronics
Tool:	Issues Communication

Lesson: Apple seems to be following the same path Nike took during the 1990s. Without effectively analyzing the issues involved in its downstream supply chain, Apple appears to be experiencing crises resulting from simmering issues in its manufacturing plants.

(*Continued*)

(*Continued*)

for Apple. The apparent cause of the explosion was improper ventilation in a metal polishing shop following an explosion triggered by dust buildup. Critics had also cited the high suicide rate at the Chengdu plant. They claimed Apple had ignored these issues and not monitored its supply chains and conditions in international plants to prevent crises from suddenly occurring.

Another issue was "simmering" in Apple's business environment. When Apple's iPad was publically announced in January 2010 and released to customers in April 2010, it was an instant success. Apple sold nearly 15 million devices globally before the end of 2010. The sustainable push of many governments, businesses, and institutions to reduce the amount of printed paper is growing into a megatrend. Medical centers are moving from paper records of patient information and physical copies of x-rays toward all electronic or digitized record keeping. University classrooms likewise are moving toward use of tablet devices and away from printed books. Martinez-Estrada and Conaway[15] asserted "that before the year 2015 the eReader will be the largest platform used in university education."

For manufacturers of tablet devices, a threat (or issue leading to a crisis) becomes immediately apparent. The issue for makers of the Kindle, Nook, or iPad is the *threat of substitute products.* A legal crisis developed for Apple in September 2011, when Samsung released its Galaxy tablet device, which was based on Google's Android operating system. A newer version of Samsung's device, the Galaxy Tab 10.1, began selling in 2011. It functioned and looked much like the iPad, so Apple brought lawsuits against Samsung. The legal struggle began in the U.S., continued in Australia, and spread globally. Eventually, Samsung was allowed to continue sales of the Tab 10.1, but critics claimed Samsung waited until the iPad was released and then copied iPad functions without violating intellectual copyright.[16]

Issues, threats, and challenges must be identified before the crisis communication strategy can be addressed. How can you identify and rank strategic matters currently existing in your business? These issues that are not yet crises may be identified in relationship to stakeholders, including customers and employees, activists, and nongovernmental organizations. Potential issues may focus on employee rights, labor unions, diversity, cultural competence, immigrant documentation, workplace violence, or factory working conditions. Other issues may be related to the environmental impact of your products or services or the sustainability image of your company. These issues may be "simmering" and destined to evolve into a crisis.

Most material published today focuses on management of issues and crises, not on communication. We make one final point about issue management before we proceed to a discussion of communication in crises. If your company is not satisfied with its issue management, good methods are available for prioritizing and quantifying strategic issues. Igor Ansoff[17] called the strategic issue "a forthcoming development, either inside or outside of the organization, which is likely to have an important impact on the ability of the enterprise to meet its objectives."[18] Through his work in the European Institute for Advanced Studies in Management, Brussels, Belgium, he has helped company's prepare for crises. Ansoff developed a Strategic Issue Management (SIM) system, which is a methodical procedure to identify important trends and events internal and external to the company. He suggests a procedure for prioritizing these trends and events and a method for responding quickly. It is beyond the scope of this chapter to discuss how to quantitatively assess issues and to address this SIM tool in-depth, but we recommend consulting the Ansoff source. The key idea is that issues currently existing in the firm's external environment must be assessed and identified to effectively prepare for crises.

Crisis Communication

Even though organizations complete good strategic plans, conduct accurate internal assessments of their core strengths, and evaluate the external social and environmental conditions, the organization may still make mistakes when communicating during crises. Company representatives, for example, typically do not answer questions that stakeholders and the public are asking. The organization may not communicate right away and will delay its response. Communication becomes confusing when different stories are released. Or perhaps communication seems incomplete when partial information is released and the public expected full disclosure of the crisis events. Such mistakes can be avoided by effectively communicating according to a well prepared crisis plan. The following case illustrates an appropriate response to a sudden crisis.

Domino's Pizza

Company:	Domino's Pizza
Industry:	Fast Food
Tool:	Crisis Communication

In April 2009 two employees in a North Carolina Domino's Pizza store posted a YouTube video showing that they themselves were contaminating food while it was being prepared. Various "gross" things were done to the food in the video,

Lesson: The excellent response by Patrick Doyle, President of Domino's Pizza, serves as a model for companies in crisis. His use of online media to reply to a crisis posted on YouTube seemed to mediate the impact of the crisis.

including sneezing on the food and placing vile bodily fluids in it before the food was sent out to customers. Immediately, the YouTube video went viral on the internet. When Patrick Doyle, President of Domino's Pizza, learned of the video, he called in a camera crew and posted his own two-minute response on YouTube. His actions were highly unusual because his immediate response preceded major media coverage. He in essence helped shift media attention from the defamatory video to his own response.

The apology in a crisis is crucial. At the beginning of Doyle's YouTube message, he sincerely apologized for the employee incident and thanked the members of the online community who had alerted him about the video, thus allowing Domino's to take action. Key facts about the incident appeared in his message. He stated that the two Domino's employees had been dismissed, and felony warrants were issued for their arrest. Their store had been shut down and sanitized. Domino's response proved to be a good one.

Along with the timing and the apology, Doyle demonstrated a consistent, positive, and empathetic tone throughout his message. He said "there is nothing more important or sacred to us than our customers'

(Continued)

trust." He said he was not surprised that so much damage had been done to the Domino's brand, but it "sickened" him how the actions of two employees had impacted Domino's great system, the 125,000 men and women of who work for independent business owners in 60 countries around the world. Finally, his closing remarks focused on regaining customer confidence and trust: Domino's takes "tremendous pride in crafting delicious food that is delivered to you every day and ... we want to thank you for hanging in there with us as we work to regain your trust."

How was the Domino's brand affected? As expected, the brand quality and buzz ratings were negatively affected initially, as measured by BrandIndex.[19] Through prompt action, the company communicated effectively, ensured the safety of its customers, regained their trust and confidence, and preserved the reputation of the Domino's brand. In addition to the YouTube response, Dominos also used Twitter to take advantage of this social media to help mediate the crisis.

The CCP

Do you think BP followed a CCP? In a recent survey by the Foundation for Public Affairs, "81 percent of the companies surveyed indicated they had a formalized crisis management plan. While most companies are preparing for crises, their degree of preparedness varies widely."[20] We acknowledge that communicating during a crisis is indeed difficult. Someone once said that it is like "putting lipstick on a pig." If BP did have a plan, for instance, its communication was severely criticized for the lack of public information it released about the amount of oil spilled in the Gulf and the extent of damage done to the environment.

The extensive Deepwater Horizon oil spill in the Gulf of Mexico was an unprecedented event for BP. It created havoc for businesses along the coastline of the U.S., and disrupted the lives and livelihoods of thousands of coastal residents who are still recovering from the impact. Consider the suddenness of the disaster. When the deep water drilling rig exploded, an immediate crisis occurred with 11 people killed and 17 others injured. While the explosion with its immediate human toll was horrific, few people anticipated the full extent of the second crisis when the resulting oil spill disrupted the ecosystem of the region which directly impacted the seafood industry and tourism along the Gulf coast. BP was faced with responding in a way that could make amends for the tremendous human and economic losses and also prove strategically beneficial to preserving their business reputation.

Is an apology important? Freeo[21] offered the following advice: "One thing to remember that is crucial in a crisis is tell it all, tell it fast and tell the truth. If you do this you have done all you can to minimize the situation." And an apology in the message may be appropriate. It's best to admit what has happened. In fact, we adopt the advice of the ERC, which recommends that corporations communicate, communicate, communicate "and follow 'the Three As' – Acknowledge, Apologize, Act." These familiar 3 A's of customer service are appropriately applied to crisis communication.

John Greenwood[22] emphasized in a *Wall Street Journal* article that unreserved apologies are absolutely crucial to effective communication. The role of the CEO is becoming more important when communicating the apology and the message must contain "balanced contrition" with statements that point to the root of the problem and state how the problem will be corrected. Although apologies are important to communicate, "sorry" often is not enough. Greenwood[23] stressed that Nike, Toyota, BP, and Domino's Pizza learned the difficult lesson that "brand risk is a key threat to a company's license to do business." The business must apologize expediently in a crisis, but in the long term it must also take steps to repair its brand.

We discussed earlier in this chapter that strategic issues should be identified and assessed before the organization is ready to prepare a communication crisis plan. If a decision has been made by top management to create a plan and use it, crisis preparation can begin. Decision makers can tap into good resources, such as the consultant group Lexicon Communications <www.crisismanagement.com>, which claims to be the nation's oldest and most experienced crisis management firm, specializing in crisis communication. The Wilson Group <www.wilson-group.com> also specializes in "real world" crisis management and media training.

Stages in a CCP

The purpose of a CCP is twofold. First, a good plan helps moderate or temper the effects of a crisis. Second, it primarily provides a way to ensure safety for employees, customers, and other stakeholders. The CCP requires intensive, internal communication among all departments and areas of the business, and it generally moves through the following stages illustrated in Figure 4.2.

1. **Begin with Top Management**. The CCP begins at the top and moves down the organization. It should be conceived and supported by top management. A crisis team cannot be created solely "as a good idea" to be adopted by upper management and employees. It requires the president, CEO, or Board to fully own the plan and allocate to the team necessary time and resources to complete its work. When a decision is made to implement a CCP within the organization, the Board can bring personnel onto the crisis team.

2. **Create a Crisis Team**. The crisis team is not a voluntary project group and requests for participation may draw little interest. The president or CEO must appoint personnel to be part of the team and include key individuals such as chief of security, information technology director, director of media relations, and appropriate vice

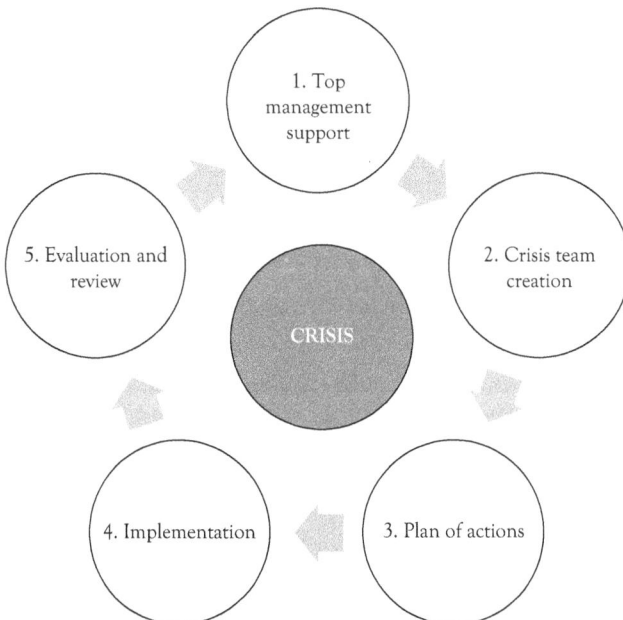

Figure 4.2. Stages of the CCP (adapted from Barton 1993).

presidents or senior managers. An attorney or legal advisor may be selected to join the crisis team. The Board may want to appoint core team members and ask other individuals to join depending on the type of crisis. If an industrial accident occurs, for example, technicians may need to meet with the team. Once the core team is established, the CEO should designate (appoint) one individual to direct the group and become point person. This person should have full authority to make decisions. If there is turnover of personnel on the core team, members with seniority may help newcomers with the transition and keep institutional knowledge.

Updated, specific contact information, including cell phones and email addresses, should be exchanged among team members when the team is created. Ultimately, the designated leader has primary authority and will serve as crisis contact person. Contact information that may be private should be kept within team membership. The leader may also be the one who speaks to the public and provides crucial information to the media if the CEO is not chosen.

All these decisions are made when creating the crisis team. The team leader will ultimately determine the significance of the crisis and decide, in consultation with the team, whether the CCP should be implemented. The team will also draw up a fact sheet about determining the cause of the event. Remember, the purpose of the team is not to identify types of crises, anticipate threats or challenges, or foresee events that may impact business. The goal is to develop a communication plan to put into action once the crisis occurs.

3. **Establish a plan of action and procedures**. This "decision tree" of personnel will be the basis of effective communication in the CCP. All personnel should represent appropriate areas of the business and have specific individuals with whom they report, including vice presidents, senior managers, the director of PR, and director of IT.

   The CCP should provide a list of individuals who will be contacted immediately. The plan should indicate which communication channels are used, such as texting, cell phone, or home phone. Many crisis planners believe the president or the CEO should make the first public announcement, and whoever is designated should be clearly stated in the CCP. The plan should list the contact person for the media and identify the office where calls should be directed. Journalists who try to contact employees for interviews may ask nonauthorized personnel to field questions. The plan should require all employees to direct all calls and interviews to a central person or office.

Procedures will involve both internal and external communication. Internally, the team leader may communicate immediately with the chief of security, who will be incharge of safely locking down the building or plant facility. This lockdown is critical in the event of a chemical spill, explosion, or employee violence. Safe zones should be established and instructions given on how to go to safe zones. This security chief will first ensure safety of employees and customers who still may be in the facility. The team leader may next communicate with the media relations director who will disseminate information quickly among managers and directors internally. The next person in the communication list may be the director of technology, who will coordinate postings of information on the company web site or update blog information. This order of contact should be established in the CCP.

Externally, media relations will contact radio and television stations and may be responsible for writing actual messages to be released to the public. A list of community leaders and government officials may be listed in the plan.

4. **Plan implemented and pilot tested**. The writing of a communication crisis plan will of course go through several revisions before it is officially completed, and the plan will most likely require formal approval and signatories. The plan should be implemented and pilot tested through a simulation once the necessary approval is obtained. An actual test should be conducted within the business.

Begin by announcing that a simulation of the communication plan will be conducted and designate a certain day and time. The announcement or memorandum should be sent to all areas and personnel. Internal communication will be intensive at this point. The planning team may also want to recommend a system of emergency alerts to notify employees. If so, that system should be tested during the simulation. Communication channels must be verified, including cell phone numbers, texting numbers, and email addresses of key individuals and contact personnel. How often should the tests be conducted? Many companies chose once or twice a year. The frequency will be based on recommendations of the crisis team.

The written communication plan is much like an architectural drawing of a building that must be adjusted during the construction of the building. The formal written CCP plan will be introduced to the company and tested, but it will probably be adjusted or "refined" after an actual test. The written plan is implemented, pilot tested, evaluated, and revised. In this sense the CCP is a "living document" because it will be constantly updated and revised.

Finally, the CCP must provide a system of formal training for employees about procedures to follow during a crisis. The Board must allow time and designate resources and most likely, the department of Human Resources will conduct training. If necessary, key employees may be given a title or position to represent their status during the crisis. An individual may be placed in charge of a floor or department when a crisis event happens. That person will be designated as the one to contact for information or to give directions.

5. **Evaluation, review, and follow up**. Evaluation and review of a CCP will be ongoing, but especially important at two different points in its implementation. The first important evaluation occurs immediately after the plan is pilot tested. When the simulation is run for the first time, many communication weaknesses may be revealed. The crisis team should meet within one or two weeks and evaluate the effectiveness of the trial. A set of evaluation metrics or rubrics may be included in the original CCP. If not, the crisis team may use its own metrics. Key evaluation questions will center on internal vulnerabilities and the degree of risk. Risk factors and areas of risk will be noted by crisis team.

The second important evaluation and review happens after the crisis itself. Everything about preparedness and communication should be assessed, especially contact with key stakeholders. The crisis team must develop a time line for working through the aftermath of the crisis. Internal communication will remain intensive, and external communication will equally continue with stakeholders.

Crisis Ethics

Companies in times of crisis are under great public scrutiny. Any ethical misbehavior in times of crisis has the potential to magnify the severity of a crisis situation. Thus, crisis ethics are a crucial factor for successfully coping with crises. The ethical decision by Maple Leaf Foods CEO to respond quickly and openly on public media demonstrated high standards in acceptance of responsibility and transparency when communicating the message. Similarly, the decision by the CEO of Domino's Pizza also demonstrated responsibility and openness. When a company decides beforehand it will communicate its values to stakeholders, its chances of weathering crisis greatly improve. It may even be better positioned at the end of the crisis than at the beginning.

The ERC[24] defines ethics as "**Ethics pertains to situations where 'the right thing to do' is in question, and the outcome of the decision affects other people.** Because every answer in a crisis has an impact on others, every question is at least partly about ethics."

We summarize this section with a quote from the ERC that keeps our focus on ethics during a crisis: "The consistent lodestone throughout a crisis is ethical behavior – openness to the truth, acceptance of responsibility, and a commitment to setting things right. Both experience and empirical data support this advice. Companies with ethical cultures, beginning with strong tone at the top, fare better in day to day operations and during crisis."[25]

Conclusion

The goal of a CCP is to minimize the negative impact of a crisis and to ensure safety of those involved. A good plan will provide order and help achieve these two goals. Rumors fly and emotions run high in a chaotic environment. Anxiety and misinformation may linger for months or years after a crisis. A strong CCP allows the business to be prepared and ready to act when the crisis happens.

CHAPTER 5

Communicating Through Institutional Documents: Vision, Mission, and Codes of Conduct

A key purpose of vision and mission statements is to inform stakeholders of what the firm is, what it seeks to accomplish, and show it seeks to serve.[1]

Management tools exist today which are commonplace and ones that companies use to communicate their commitment to sustainability. We cover three of these tools in this chapter, including vision and mission statements, tools which are carefully drafted by top management and provide long-term guidance through strategic planning and performance. Codes of conduct represent a third tool that guides a company's ethical and sustainable behavior. We begin the chapter with a discussion of vision statements incorporating several examples. Next, we look at mission statements and the purpose they serve. Finally, we focus on codes of conduct, a less discussed tool in sustainability performance but nevertheless important in communicating sustainability in the supply chain. First, let's look into the German company of Bayerische Motoren Werke AG (BMW).

BMW AG, founded in 1917 and one of Germany's largest industrial companies, manufactures well-known automotive brands, BMW, MINI and Rolls-Royce, and produces a high quality line of motorcycles. The

Company: BMW AG
Industry: Automotive
Lesson: A successful company economically and a leader in the automotive industry, BMW exhibits how economic and environmental bottom grow together. The company's mission and vision statement communicates its sustainability performance.

(Continued)

(*Continued*)

company employs nearly 100,000 people globally, maintains a network of 25 production and assembly plants, and owns 43 sales subsidiaries.[2] Significantly, BMW's sustainability performance earned it a number one rating in the Automobile & Parts supersector within the Dow Jones classification. The company's combined sustainability scores on the economic, social, and environments dimensions earned it the exemplary rating, demonstrating why it is considered a sustainability leader.

Having been branded as a sustainable company, BMW also made advances throughout its value chain. The company in 2010 presented a fuel-cell-powered hybrid vehicle, and development of electrically powered cars is underway through the Megacity Vehicle project, which is identified as Project i. The vehicles are expected to have a range of 100 miles and a top speed of 95 miles per hour. Furthermore, BMW made significant advances in reducing environmental impact in the component production process by reducing organic elements in exhaust air by 98 percent and aligning its operations with mandatory requirements for environmental and social sustainability.[3] BMW continues to make efforts to hire employees for its sustainable business growth, offering competitive wages and employee training in sustainable business. In a key report, BMW AG board member Frank-Peter Arndt stated "Between autumn 2009 and summer 2011, some 2,450 employees took part in sustainability-specific training."[4]

Interestingly, the mission statement of the BMW Group does not address sustainability issues. The mission asserts the company "is the world's leading provider of premium products and premium services for individual mobility."[5] This statement defines the company up to the year 2020. Absent the sustainability focus in its mission, the company still is a highly ranked sustainability company. Its vision also is stated succinctly and clearly yet does not address sustainability: To become the most successful premium manufacturer in the car industry. Vision and missions statement provide important long-term direction of companies, especially in moving toward becoming a sustainability company. Despite BMW's mission and vision not giving clear direction to its sustainability performance, the company continues to make progress in sustainability development and receive high ratings.

Vision Statements

The vision statement reflects the long-term strategy of a company and expresses what it wants to become in the future. The vision gives the big picture and expresses the company's purpose and direction. Such statements usually are worded simply and form the foundation for CSR performance. Worded carefully, the vision may demonstrate to stakeholders the company's CSR commitment. Thus, the vision statement is the beginning for effective CSR performance.

As the world's largest consumer packaged goods company, Procter and Gamble's (P&G) environmental vision statement stemmed from its global vision statement, "Be, and be recognized as, the best consumer products and services company in the world."[6] Interestingly, this vision does not refer to sustainability. The phrase "the best" gives a qualitative dimension to the vision expresses the company's purpose and long-term goal, and emphasizes business leadership qualities. Although this vision tells the "heart" of P&G, it does not express the tone or direction for sustainability performance. Vision statements do not change much while mission statements may be modified based on competitive environment conditions.

Coca Cola versus PepsiCo Coca Cola, the world's largest beverage company, came in second in sustainability, according to the Dow Jones Sustainability Index. PepsiCo ranked first over Coca Cola in sustainability performance in the Food & Beverage supersector. Both companies stress sustainability in their vision statements. Coca Cola's vision emphasizes that it will "...continue achieving sustainable, quality growth" with people, portfolios, partners, planet, profit, and productivity.[7] PepsiCo's vision seeks "to continually improve all aspects of the world in which we operate—environment, social, economic—creating a better tomorrow than today," a vision appropriately called *Performance with Purpose.*[8] Despite the two similar visions, PepsiCo exhibited stronger sustainability progress. In May 2011, Coca Cola CEO Muhtar Kent announced that Coca Cola "took an important and exciting step in its sustainability journey by announcing the formation of a new global Office of Sustainability led by Bea Perez," who is Coca Cola's first Chief Sustainability Officer.[9] Perhaps this important announcement may propel Coca Cola to first place in the Dow Jones Sustainability Index (DJSI) rating.

A clear vision is essential for the future, especially when organizations are implementing planned change such as a new social or environmental program. However, one of the most frequently encountered problems is communicating vision.[10] Indeed, creating shared understanding among employees of what the organization wants to become can be difficult. Rogers, Gunesekera, and Yang[11] suggest several ways management can use language to communicate effectively, and we adapt these ways to writing a vision statement. First, identify, name, and order topics of managerial concern. Managers must choose whether the central topics are sustainability, customer service, social enrichment, or economic growth. Second, mangers must realize how important selection of words and arrangement of the sentence can count. Third, managers must carefully select adjectives, adverbs, and verbs of the vision statement. Use terms like global, innovative, quality, and commitment selectively.

P&G announced via webcast on September 27, 2010, a new sustainability vision.[12] The webcast emphasized company-wide goals "using 100% renewable or recycled materials for all products and packaging, powering our plants with 100% renewable energy, having zero consumer or manufacturing waste go to landfills …"[13] The most interesting part of the announcement was the specific 2020 deadline P&G set for completion of the sustainability goals, which most large multinational enterprises typically do not establish. Giving details of the goals, P&G stated specific percentages for improvement of its products and operations, using the year 2010 as a baseline. Such bold leadership stemmed from a strong, sustainable vision and set high sustainable standards for competitors in the consumer packaged goods industry.

Another global leader in sustainability follows a vision statement stressing the future and the customer. Toyota's global vision integrates responsibility wording and expresses how the company leads "the way to the future of mobility, enriching lives around the world with the safest and most responsible ways of moving people."[14] Visser and Tolhurst[15] reported significant gains by Toyota toward this vision. During 1997 and 2007 the company had "improved the average fuel efficiency of its cars in Japan, the US and Europe by 17.4%."[16] Sales of hybrid cars continue to rise significantly in these areas. Toyota also uses the term "philosophy" when referring to its vision statement. Country by country vision statements vary slightly but align with the global vision. The vision statement for the U.S. Toyota is stated, "to be the most successful and respected car company in America."[17] Thus, Toyota's leadership in the automotive industry reflects a strong, sustainable vision.

Other companies state their sustainability performance visions less directly than P&G and Toyota. Walmart publishes its global mission as "we save people money so they can live better,"[18] the identical goal that founder Sam Walton envisioned when Walmart was started. The company also states its sustainability mission indirectly as "being an efficient and profitable business and being a good steward of the environment …"[19] Its broad environmental goals have no specific deadline attached. For example, Walmart wants "to be supplied 100 percent by renewable energy, to create zero waste, to sell products that sustain people and the environment,"[20] but gives no timeline for accomplishing these goals.

Put into Practice!

Read the vision statements on the left and write the name of the company we discussed in the preceding section in the right column. (1) P&G, (2) Coca Cola, (3) PepsiCo, (4), Toyota USA. In the third column, state how well you believe the company integrates sustainability into the vision and rate its wording (+=excellent, 0=average, – =poor).

Vision statement	Company	Analyze sustainability wording
the way to the future of mobility, enriching lives around the world with the safest and most responsible ways of moving people		
…continue achieving sustainable, quality growth with people, portfolios, partners, planet, profit, and productivity.		
to continually improve all aspects of the world in which we operate—environment, social, economic—creating a better tomorrow than today,		
Be, and be recognized as, the best consumer products and services company in the world		

Answers: Toyota, Coca Cola, PepsiCo, P&G.

When companies work through the process of writing a strategic management plan, the vision and mission statements tend to be developed first and guide the remainder of the plan. The mission statement specifically tends to be readjusted or recalibrated based on stakeholder expectations and feedback,[21] but not the vision. The vision and mission statements are important communication tools with stakeholders, who can learn a lot about the company from these statements. The vision statement is typically written by the CEO or top leadership because of its enduring importance. The mission statement derives from the vision and is adjusted as often as required.

Mission Statements

Mission statements define the purpose of the business in the competitive environment in which it exists. These statements communicate which customers the business intends to serve (Hitt, Ireland, & Hoskisson, 2011). The mission statement is more concrete than the vision statement and it tells stakeholders *who the company is* and *what it does*.[22] P&G's mission statement clearly defines its business, "We will provide branded products and services of superior quality and value that improve the lives of the world's consumers, now and for generations to come."[23] Similarly, Toyota's mission for the US tells what its company is and what it does, "to attract and attain customers with high-valued products and services and the most satisfying ownership experience in America."[24]

Sustainability mission statements also exist in organizations dedicated to learning and education. Textbook publishers differentiate their markets through mission statements. U.S. publisher Cengage developed a lengthy mission statement inclusive of sustainability and establishing clear differentiation with competitors. The company "is to be the most respected and innovative source of teaching, learning, and research solutions for the academic, professional, and library markets worldwide. We are leading the transition from print to value-added digital and custom solutions by developing a deep understanding of our customers' needs, capitalizing on synergies across our businesses and delivering innovative products and services that cannot be matched by our competitors…"[25] Similarly, Business Expert Press, headquartered in New York, provides low-cost digital and paper text solutions for students. These sustainable mission statements by publishers illustrate the importance of digital solutions as a significant step toward a reduced environmental footprint in the classroom.

In the preceding mission statements, which seems most sustainable? What content should a mission statement contain? Williams[26] reviews a variety of experts for recommended content and surprisingly found close similarity among the recommendations. Pearce and David,[27] an often cited source, recommended eight key components in the written mission statement. These are important guidelines that are worth following and we discuss them in the following table, including a ninth component added by David.[28]

Table 5.1 lists nine content components compiled by Williams (2008) and appropriate questions related to each component in column 2. Interestingly, none of the recommended components identify sustainability, although most companies today incorporate sustainability into the mission statement. It is important to note that not all of these components must be included in mission statements. The idea is to select content areas important to the company strategy. The mission statement will emphasize customer relationships, for example, as a business strengthens its customer orientation. Because sustainability was omitted as a component, we added column 3 to suggest questions focusing on sustainability. The components are not ordered in priority or alphabetized.

The banking sector exhibits how several of these content components are included in a mission statement. Westpac Banking Corp. earned the Dow Jones Sustainability Index's top rating in their listing of the banking supersector. Westpac bank primarily serves Australia, New Zealand, and the Pacific islands. It employees approximately 38,000 people and in 2010, the bank generated 32.9 billion Australian dollars. Westpac publishes its mission as a way "to earn all its customers' business." The bank elaborates on this mission by stating it "is aimed at building deep and enduring customer relationships—such that customers stay with us, conduct more business with us and recommend us to others. We seek to meet our customers' total banking and wealth needs and earn all of their business."[29] This mission statement integrates several of the components we discussed: customers, products and services, philosophy, and concern for public image. The bank's vision statement of course is less specific, "to be one of the world's

Table 5.1. Recommended Content Components for Mission Statements

Component	William's (2008) question	Sustainability content
1. Customers	Who are the enterprise's customers?	Who are the stakeholders (including customers) buying products with sustainability features?
2. Products or services	What are the firm's major products or services?	Do our products or services reflect sustainable practices?
3. Location	Where does the firm compete?	How do transportation and distribution systems affect environmental footprints and what are the work local social standards?
4. Technology	What is the firm's basic technology?	How does our firm's technology negatively or positively s contribute to sustainable development?
5. Concern for survival	What is the firm's commitment to economic objectives?	Are economic objectives balanced with social and environmental objectives to ensure sustainability of the overall system?
6. Philosophy	What are the basic beliefs, values, aspirations, and philosophical priorities of the firm?	Do basic beliefs, values and aspirations reflect sustainable philosophy?
7. Self concept	What are the firm's major strengths and competitive advantages?	What are our core strengths in sustainability?
8. Concern for public image	What are the firm's public responsibilities, and what image is desired?	What are our social responsibilities and our desired sustainable image?
9. Concern for employees	What is the firm's attitude toward its employees?	Does our firm seek employees experienced in sustainability and provide training in sustainability?

Source: Adapted from Williams (2008, p. 109).

great companies, helping our customers, communities and people to prosper and grow," but still aligns with its mission statement.[30]

Several reasons exist why Westpac bank's sustainability performance ranked first in the global banking sector of the Dow Jones Sustainability Index.[31] First, the firm demonstrated unique leadership by positioning sustainability as a priority in its long-term strategy, and it had exhibited exceptional stakeholder management with these sustainability issues. Second, Westpac mainstreamed sustainability by integrating environmental, social, and governmental (ESG) concerns into its financial product development. Third, the firm recognized that its societal impact and environmental impact came from the organization's lending practices and investment decisions. Additionally, Westpac was making progress in reporting on social and environmental performance metrics. All of these reasons explain Westpac's rating, and importantly it reveals a bank with a strong commitment toward becoming a sustainability organization. Without effective communication in each area, Westpac performance would be little known outside the organization itself.

Other companies also illustrate sustainability in their mission statements. Itaúsa-Investimentos Itau, a Brazilian investor relations firm headquartered in Sao Paulo, Brazil, employs 125,000 people and operates an extensive network of 4900 branches and 34,000 banking service centers in Brazil.[32] Itau's purpose on sustainability "orients, encourages and supports the companies in their efforts to integrate the topic of sustainability into their business development processes." The DJSI rated this investment firm high because of its commitment to align social, cultural, and environmental practices to create value for society "within a chain of wealth sharing." We extensively discuss in Chapter 6 on sustainability reporting how Itaúsa made a commitment to disclosing its sustainability performance according to the Global Reporting Initiative (GRI) guidelines. In fact, each paragraph in the annual report displays its GRI rating, a reporting process that follows GRI guidelines.

South Korean Lotte Shopping Co. provides another excellent example of a responsible mission statement in a highly rated sustainable company. According to its annual report, the large retailer is number one in the retail industry in Asia and number one in sustainability in the world in the Retail Supersector (Lotte Annual Report, 2010). Lotte has managed to gain an advantage over competitors by "exhibiting unparalleled commitment to social and environmental issues."[33] The company's 2011 annual sustainability report states its mission as a commitment, "Lotte Shopping brings innovative customer and brand value through unrivalled service and merchandising. We drive a broad commitment to sustainability and actively engage ourselves in a wide range of social-contribution activities across environmental and social spectrum."[34] Lotte

(Continued)

(Continued)

is a participant and stakeholder of the United Nations Global Compact and qualifies for the Global Compact active level. The retailer's self-assessment expresses continued support for the 10 principles of the compact. Lotte has reported actions or relevant policies related to human rights, labor, environment, and anticorruption. The firm's reports include measurements of outcomes of its sustainability performance.[35]

Put into Practice!

Understanding what other companies say in their mission statements may help us write our own. Read the mission statements on the left and write the name of the company we discussed in the right column, **(1) BMW AG, (2) Cengage, (3) Walmart, (4) P&G, or (5) Toyota USA.** Identify components from Table 5.1 and write the component in the right column

Mission statement	Company	What components (Table 5.1) appear in statement?
We will provide branded products and services of superior quality and value that improve the lives of the world's consumers, now and for generations to come		
To be the most respected and innovative source of teaching, learning and research solutions for the academic, professional and library markets worldwide		
We save people money so they can live better		
The world's leading provider of premium products and premium services for individual mobility		
To attract and attain customers with high-valued products and services and the most satisfying ownership experience in America		

Company Answers: P&G, Cengage, Walmart, BMW, Toyota.

Codes of Conduct

The third key management tool for communicating sustainability through institutional documents is Codes of Conduct. *Codes* represent a set of sustainability standards for behavior within a company and these standards govern relationships with various stakeholders. Codes of conduct differ from codes of ethics, which generally express values and broader ethical guidelines. Likewise, corporate polices establish broader regulations, while codes of conduct set specific standards for company behavior. Walmart, for example, released its ethical sourcing standards in 2007 in the form of 15 questions for suppliers.[36] The questions were later revised into 13 categories addressing sustainability issues, ranging from compliance with labor laws to financial integrity. As one of the largest companies in the world, Walmart and its well-known standards exert a tremendous influence on its supply chain. Thousands of businesses must conform to their sustainability standards to do business with Walmart.

Walmart's codes of conduct are but one part of its total sustainability performance. Preuss[37] showed how codes of conduct in large companies, particularly in the London stock exchange (FTSE100 constituent companies), reflect only part of the sustainability approach of businesses. In other words, a strong code of conduct does not guarantee sustainable business performance. Other broader codes established by a company also direct sustainability, including codes from government legislation, antitrust law, human rights, and international norms and standards, each of which set social and environmental business performance.[38] Codes exist as an important management tool that communicates to stakeholders the desired social and environmental behaviors of key stakeholders.

What content should codes of conduct contain? Netherland researchers conducted an assessment of codes of conduct in Amsterdam and provided several indicators for writing different codes.[39] Their research assessment was based on four assumptions about codes, which we believe provide good guidelines for content requirements in a code of conduct. Table 5.2 lists these guidelines.

Table 5.2. Content Guidelines for Codes of Conduct

• The code contains both open guidelines about desirable behavior (value orientation) and closed guidelines pointing at prohibited behavior (compliance orientation)
• The code relates both to the behavior of individual employees and to the collective behavior of the organization as a whole
• The code indicates how responsibility is distributed within the firm
• The code is used as an instrument for enhancing CSR

Source: Adapted from Nijhof et al. (2003, p. 66).

If we examine Walmart's code of conduct, we see all four content guidelines reflected in their standards, assuming the last guideline is met by Walmart's enhancement and improvement of CSR with suppliers.

One organization establishes global standards for codes of conduct. The Ethical Trading Initiative (ETI) exists as an alliance of companies, trade unions, and voluntary organizations that sets internationally recognized codes of labor practice founded upon conventions of the International Labour Organisation. ETI's Base Code covers nine categories of labor practice.[40] Nike has established a well-known code of conduct which sets specific behaviors expected of its supply chain factories. Nike's code begins with the statement, "At Nike, we believe that although there is no finish line, there is a clear starting line.[41] The company makes a clear break with the past difficulties in sustainability performance by beginning its code of conduct with this theme. Today, Nike is recognized as a leader in responsibility, and the company binds contract factories to specific minimum behaviors of conduct, including voluntary employment, minimum age standards, and healthy and safe working environment. Interestingly, Nike's code follows the content guidelines discussed earlier. The code contains desirable behavior standards and closed guidelines about prohibited behavior, and it addresses individual employee behavior and organizations as a whole. Nike states, "It is our intention to use these standards as an integral component to how we approach NIKE, Inc. sourcing strategies, how we evaluate factory performance, and how we determine with which factories Nike will continue to engage and grow our business."[42] Clearly, the responsibility for enforcing the code of conduct lies with Nike itself.

Put it to practice! The code of conduct for BMW appears below. Analyze BMW's code according the four components in Table 5.2 in the right column.	Write your analysis in this column:
These guidelines are not exhaustive, and may not address all manner of offensive behavior. As such, BMW NA shall have full discretion to address any behavior that they feel is inappropriate.	
Your access to Performance Central is a privilege. BMW NA reserves the right to suspend an individual's access to the forum indefinitely at any time for reasons that include, but are not necessarily limited to, failure to abide by these guidelines. BMW NA reserves the right to delete content posted in any section of Performance Central that it deems inappropriate at any time for any reason. BMW NA reserves the right to evaluate each incident on a case by case basis.	
Guidelines: • No profanity. • No harassment or discrimination. • No derogatory terms against a person, race, culture, group or organization. • No threats or defamatory language. • No advertising or soliciting. • No selling or trading. • No spamming or excessive off-topic threads. • No sexually offensive materials. • No forgery or impersonation.	

Summary

This chapter illustrated how three important management tools commonly used today in business, vision statements, mission statements, and codes of conduct, serve a significant purpose in shaping the ultimate sustainability performance of a company. Visions statements, which reflect the long-term strategy of a company, express what the firm wants to become in the future and must become more than a piece of paper on the shelf.

The mission statement is a second management tool that defines the purpose of a business in its competitive environment and reflects which customers the business intends to serve. Generally, the mission statement is less enduring than the vision statement and more concrete in its wording. We suggested that the content of mission statements include certain components of information, including customers, products or services, location, and concern for employees.

Finally, codes of conduct represent a management tool that establishes sustainability standards for behavior within a company and how these standards govern relationships with various stakeholders.

CHAPTER 6

Sustainability Reporting: Gateway to Transparency

After more than a decade in which we have seen the amount of sustainability reports grow from less than a hundred to several thousand every year, coming from more than 80 countries worldwide, we are still a long way from being able to say sustainability reporting has reached its goal...[1]

U.S. President Barack Obama's message on the White House government's website states, "Transparency promotes accountability and provides information for citizens about what their Government is doing."[2] Setting politics aside, the president's message sets a high goal for an unprecedented level in government for openness, public trust, public participation, and collaboration. We believe these same transparency principles in Barack Obama's statement apply to sustainability reporting by companies: accountability, openness, trust, participation and collaboration. The key theme of this chapter is sustainability reporting and resulting transparency.

Itaúsa Brazil. We discussed this company briefly in Chapter 5, but now our focus is on sustainability reporting. You may remember that the DJSI ranked Itaúsa-Investimentos Itau, a Brazilian company, as first in the Global Financial Services Supersector. The DJSI is significant because

Company:	Itaúsa
Industry:	Financial Services

Lesson: A global 500 company ranked first by the Dow Jones Sustainability Index in the financial services Supersector. Itaúsa closely manages and monitors sustainable development and guarantees alignment of its environmental, social and cultural actions.

(Continued)

(Continued)

it is the first index "tracking the financial performance of the leading sustainability-driven companies worldwide."[3] Itaúsa earned the
DJSI high rating in sustainability performance because of strengths
in managing and monitoring sustainable development and guaranteeing alignment of its environmental, social, and cultural actions. The
DJSI noted one additional point about Itaúsa. The company provides
financial assistance to low-income individuals, microentrepreneurs,
and very small businesses. This assistance meets an important need for
bottom-of-the-pyramid persons.

The large company illustrates excellence in sustainability reporting,
noteworthy for a large global company. CNN Money ranked Itaúsa in
the global 500 earning approximately US$27 billion in 2011.[4] Itaúsa
exists as a large conglomerate of companies in the banking and financial services sector[5] and employs approximately 125,000, operating an
extensive network of 4900 branches and 34,000 banking service centers in Brazil.[6] According to Bloomberg,[7] Itaúsa also has operations in
Portugal, the United States, Luxembourg, Argentina, Germany, and
Belgium. Even with its large operations, Itaúsa made a commitment
to disclosing its sustainability performance according to the GRI G3
guidelines and displays a GRI rating next to each paragraph in its
annual report.

Itaúsa illustrates a commitment to high transparency in reporting and follows GRI recommendations by numbering paragraphs
in its company report related to the specific GRI guideline. Beginning in 2010, each paragraph of the report registers a GRI number
to the side, which refers to the GRI G3.1 guidelines.[8] Itaúsa's 2010
annual report displays 3.1 to the side of paragraph 1, referring
to the GRI report parameters that require a company to state its
reporting period (e.g., fiscal/calendar year). GRI report param-
eter 3.13 requires companies to state their practice with seeking
external assurance for the report. Itaúsa stated in the fourth paragraph that its accounting statements were audited by Pricewater-
houseCoopers and made available to the Brazilian Securities and
Exchange Commission (CVM).

Types of Reports

Table 6.1 represents a Classification for Reporting Activities that illustrates two types of reporting, General Reports and Single Activity Reports. General Reports cover all the company's activities under one cover. Single activity reports focus on one company activity. Examples of single activities are shown in the lower right-hand box. The vertical box on the left lists different formats that reports may take. We have identified these as interactive, web based, and traditions print.

Table 6.1. Exemplary Report Classifications

Organization-wide reports		Single activity reports	
Classified by	Report examples	Classified by	Report examples
Presentation type	Print, HTML, pdf, video, flash animation	Impact type	CO_2 or diversity reports
Stakeholder interaction	Personalized versus static information retrieval	Activity or program	Volunteering or donation reports
Periodicity	Annual, biannual, a periodical	Department	Marketing ethics or human resource practices report
Organization type	Non-profit versus for profit organization report	Stakeholder	Customer or employee satisfaction report
Degree of integration	Single integrated sustainability and financial report versus separated sustainability and financial annual reports	Purpose	For internal controlling, stakeholder transparency, or as documentation for certification.

When managers think of reporting today, they may exhibit an audible sigh and give examples of difficult financial reports, accounting reports, or production process reports. They may ask, "So why add sustainability reporting to the list"? Primarily, stakeholders pressure business organizations to report on sustainable performance. Stakeholders want to know how sustainable a company is and they require performance indicators in the form of report. Stakeholders know organizations may perform socially or environmentally well, but not report the activities well. They also know some organizations engage in reporting, but are not performing what they are reporting. Either way stakeholders want to verify a firm's performance through sustainability reporting.

What organizational advantages accrue from reporting? White[9] identified three categories of benefits resulting from sustainability reporting. Organizations may receive internal, operational, and external benefits. White's source presents an excellent chapter on this topic for further investigation. Briefly, the primary internal benefit is a unified approach to management, when vision and mission statements and codes of conduct are integrated with sustainability strategies. Operational benefits occur when a company makes major improvements in energy saving, materials conservation, or water reduction. Manufacturing processes can be redesigned and packaging and products recreated in a sustainable manner. Economic and financial benefits result from these changes. Finally, sustainability reporting benefits organizations externally by enhancing the organization's reputation and brand value with its stakeholders. Stakeholders expect sustainability reporting from organizations and know the company's competitiveness depends on excellent sustainable reporting.

The GRI and Fairtrade international are two well-known organizations that have developed and published reporting guidelines for businesses. Other reporting-guideline organizations certainly exist. The Sustainability-Integrated Guidelines for Management (SIGMA), for example, was launched in 1999 by the British Standards Institution and provides "clear, practical advice to organisations to enable them to make a meaningful contribution to sustainable development."[10] SIGMA positions itself as complementing other reporting guidelines used in organizations and it focuses on existing management systems and frameworks, such as ISO 14001 and ISO 9000 series, OHSAS 18001 and AA1000 Frameworks. In the financial profession, the Sustainable Asset Management (SAM) group, an international investment boutique based in Zurich, Switzerland, partnered with the DJSI to "provide access to a benchmark that offers investors exposure to sustainability leaders in each sector around the world."[11] Likewise, the International Federation of Accountants (IFAC) developed guidelines for the accounting profession. Information about these different reporting frameworks and benchmarks is readily available via the internet. Other global reporting standards exist, but the two cases that follow highlight The GRI and Fairtrade international.

Fairtrade International is a certification organization that monitors farmers, labor organizations, and commodities such as bananas, cane sugar, cocoa, coffee, flowers, seed cotton, and tea. Fairtrade differentiates among producer organizations and product certifications. In 2010 the organization gathered data from audit reports of 869 producer organizations (96 percent of total) that were certified by Fairtrade. The organization also gathered data from certified labor organizations. All information is made public. The goal of monitoring and reporting is "transparency, openness, and information-sharing with our stakeholders and supporters."[12]

In contrast to the GRI, Fairtrade International focuses on unique sector of global reporting standards for farmers and their products. In 1997 Fairtrade Labeling Organizations (FLO) International was originally created in Bonn, Germany, uniting several labeling initiatives into one organization. In 2004 Fairtrade Standards was established to set global standards and certification. In 2010 Fairtrade was present in 63 countries and most farmers and workers whom the organization monitored lived in Tanzania. That year the organization monitored approximately 938,000 farmers who were members and approximately 163,000 workers in certified hired labor organizations, equaling a total of over 1.1 million people. When the data are made public in annual reports on the organization's website, the benchmarking promotes transparency, openness, and information sharing.

The Sekem Initiative in Egypt, meaning "vitality from the sun" illustrates an exceptional example of how Fairtrade reporting helped development of disadvantaged producers and workers in a developing country.[13] Although the organization exists as an NGO, its report-

Company:	The Sekem Initiative
Industry:	Sustainable Human development

Lesson: The organizations contributes to the comprehensive development of the individual, society, and environment. A holistic concept encompassing integrated economic, social, and cultural development forms its key vision.

ing standards are illustrated here because of the impact these standards had on the success of the initiative. In 2004 the Sekem Initiative

(Continued)

(*Continued*)

was highlighted by a social entrepreneurship case study written at the University of Navarra, IESE Business School, Barcelona, Spain.[14] Initially, the organization was birthed in the 1970s when Dr. Ibrahim Abouleish returned from Austria to his home country of Egypt. He had been head of pharmaceutical research at a university in Austria and was overwhelmed by Egyptian problems with education, overpopulation, and pollution. As a result he became founder and chairman of Sekem to help development of Egyptian society. He began by purchasing land in the desert 60 km northeast of Cairo to show how the land could be made fruitful, healthy, and environmentally friendly.

Dr. Abouleish committed to biodynamic cultivation and created a farm by planting flowers, exotic trees, and fields of herbs and drilling water wells deep into the desert sand. Many trees lined the farm to shield it against desert storms. Because the "mother farm" was started in the 1970s, organic crops and farming were considered risky with low yields and limited return. Yet Angela Hofmann, a German agrobiologist, helped the farm grow medicinal and aromatic plants and teas, which were dependable organic crops in that climate. The venture was a success. By 2003, "Egypt was the largest market for organic products in the developing world that are worth about 100 million Egypt Pounds (LE)."[15]

A guiding principle of the Sekem Initiative stated "The social framework and social conditions of cooperation between the employees should be within clear, well-defined regulations and principles allowing the establishment of a healthy society."[16] Thus, the organization was certificated by Fairtrade reporting and established standards by stipulating that traders must pay a price covering costs of sustainable production and living. The Fairtrade standards also covered other aspects of Sekem's developing business, including a premium traders must pay so producers can invest in development. Traders also were required to pay part in advance. These Fairtrade practices stemmed from the commitment Sekem made to well-defined regulations and principles allowing the establishment of a healthy society.

Several global companies illustrate reporting procedures that meet high standards according to the GRI. These featured reports can be found on the GRI site. Clorox Company in its 2011 annual report with the sustainability title, "Think Outside the Bottle," self-declared with B+ in compliance, but checked by the GRI organization.[17] To improve clarity and transparency in reporting, Clorox could place the GRI guideline number next to each individual paragraph similar to the report Itaúsa posts. Clorox indicates that all ratings have been fully met except for four partially met ratings. In exemplary fashion the company has integrated its financial, environmental, social, and governance performance in one report.

Larsen & Toubro (L&T), an engineering and construction company based in India, self-declared with A+ in compliance.[18] L&T was awarded by the Indian Chamber of Commerce (ICC) the Corporate Governance and Sustainability Vision Award 2012 in the "Sustainability Reporting" category, confirming the GRI rating. Clearly, L&T values transparency and its reports have been externally assured for authenticity for the information presented. The company acknowledges it is the first Indian company in the engineering and construction segment in India to publically report on its sustainability performance.

Munich Airport is another organization that values transparency in its sustainability reports, called "Perspectives," and a self-declared A+. Munich has combined economic, environmental, citizenship, and social responsibility factors into one report, similar to Clorox's integrated reports, recognized as one of the first airports in the world to do so. Each of these examples illustrates transparent reporting procedures and conformity to benchmarked standards. In the next section we discuss in depth the premier GRI standards for transparency in reporting.

The GRI Standard

The GRI exists as a nonprofit organization headquartered in Amsterdam and was founded in 1997. The organization aims to provide sustainability reporting guidance so that companies work together toward a sustainable global economy. Through its framework and accountability standards, GRI enables greater organizational transparency about economic, environmental, social, and governance performance.[19] GRI standards promote clarity and candidness of reporting and deliver a strong reporting framework following major scandals with Enron, WorldCom, Parmalat, and Vivendi. The mission of GRI provides "a trusted and credible framework for sustainability reporting that can be used by organizations of any size, sector, or location."[20] To accomplish this mission, GRI created and published its comprehensive Sustainability Reporting Framework, which is widely adopted around the world and provides greater transparency for organizations. Figure 6.1 summarizes major content of the G3 Sustainability Reporting Framework.

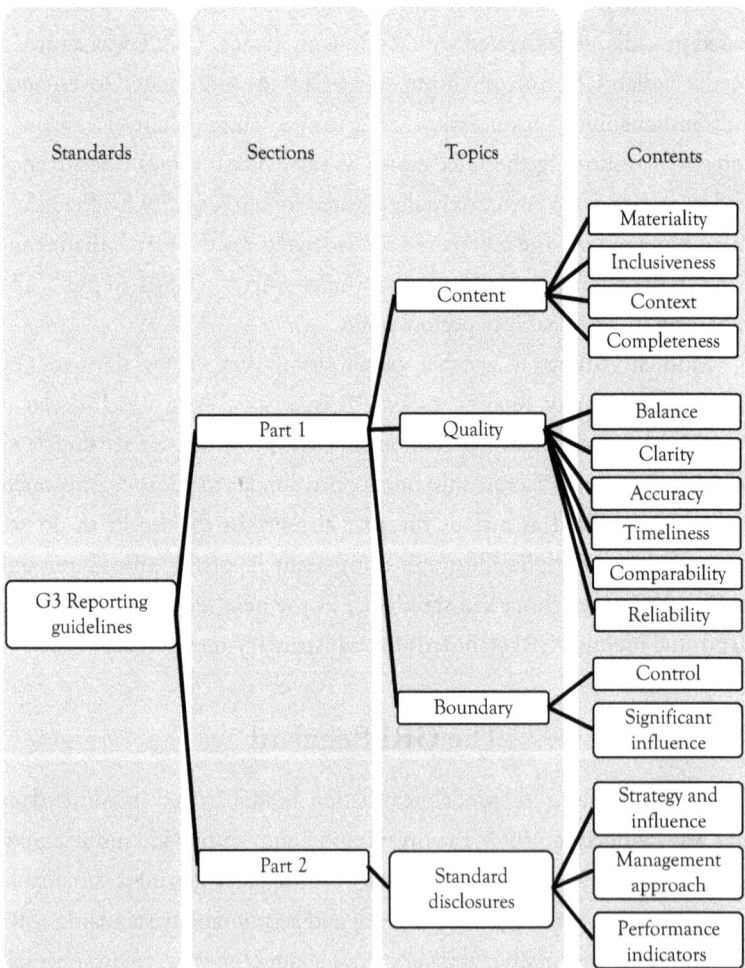

Figure 6.1. Content overview of the contents of the GRI standard.

GRI essentially defines sustainability reporting as transparency. The guidelines "turn the spotlight" on performance and require organizations to measure, disclose, and account for their sustainability activities. Stakeholders may read an organization's public reports and check how the firm performed. For example, if Nike reports it has improved working conditions in international factories, kept high standards of air quality, and ensured minimal age standards, Nike's stakeholders can verify Nike's statements. When organizations say they are following GRI standards, they are holding themselves accountable and transparent before stakeholders. GRI checks and verifies organizational reports by benchmarking data and comparing progress over time. However, stakeholder responses to the report are a true test of transparency.

Let's examine now details of GRI's reporting guidelines. The framework gives details primarily in two parts: First, Part 1 of the framework guides companies on how to report, on what content should be reported. Second, Part 2 of the framework guides companies on what to report, which is the quality of the report itself. Each part is considered of equal weight and importance with the other.

Part 1: Defining Report Content, Quality, and Boundary

The GRI framework shows the title of Part 1 as "Defining Report Content, Quality, and Boundary." We discuss this part in three sections as reporting principles for content, reporting principles for quality, and reporting guidance for boundary setting. Table 6.2 summarizes the content section. Next, we discuss six principles for defining quality following the table. The six quality principles are essentially communication principles elaborating the principles presented in Table 6.2. Finally, we briefly cover boundary setting.

The GRI framework principles presented in Table 6.2 define the sustainability report content. In summary, a company wants to "ensure a balanced and reasonable presentation of the organization's performance" by considering the materiality of the topics and indicators in the report, through stakeholder inclusiveness (identifying and responding to stakeholders), by presenting the organization's performance in the wider

Table 6.2. Part 1—Reporting Principles and Guidance

Reporting principle	Definition of principle
Materiality	The information in a report should cover topics and indicators that • reflect the organization's significant economic, environmental, and social impacts or that • would substantively influence the assessments and decisions of stakeholders and • passes the "threshold" for influencing the economic decisions of those using an organization's financial statements, investors in particular.
Stakeholder inclusiveness	The reporting organization should • identify its stakeholders and • explain in the report how it has responded to their reasonable expectations and interests.
Sustainability Context	The report should • present the organization's performance in the wider context of sustainability, • express how an organization contributes, or aims to contribute in the future, to the improvement or deterioration of economic, environmental, and social conditions, developments, and trends at the local, regional, or global level.
Completeness	The report should include • the dimensions of scope (range of sustainability topics covered in a report), boundary (range of entities, e.g., subsidiaries, joint ventures, subcontractors), and time (the need for the selected information to be complete for the time period specified by the report). • coverage of the material topics and Indicators and definition of the report boundary should be sufficient to reflect significant economic, environmental, and social impacts and enable stakeholders to assess the reporting organization's performance in the reporting period.

Source: Adapted from G3 GRI sustainability reporting guidelines.

context of sustainability, and through completeness of coverage (scope, boundary, and time).

Next, the principles in Table 6.2 are elaborated in the guidelines in a section entitled, "Reporting Principles for Defining Quality." Interestingly, these six principles for defining quality are key communication principles that guide choices on ensuring the quality of reported information and proper presentation of the report.

Reporting Principles for Defining Quality in Part 1:

- **Balancing**. One mistake companies tend to make is presenting only positive aspects of sustainability performance. When discussing the materiality of topics, for example, planners may select positive indicators and omit the negative. Or companies may be biased toward stakeholders with whom they have a positive relationship and not be inclusive of all stakeholders. Bias toward only positive performances is an easy mistake to make.

- **Comparability**. GRI guidelines serve as benchmarking data that allows companies to compare information and progress from year to year. As the guidelines state, this comparability is necessary for evaluating performance. Consistency from year to year with the Principle of Materiality, for example, can be made. Comparisons *between* companies must be done sensitively.

- **Accuracy**. The guidelines define this principle as "The reported information should be sufficiently accurate and detailed for stakeholders to assess the reporting organization's performance." We agree that accuracy of qualitative information is the degree of clarity, detail, and balance in presentation. This information must meet the sufficiency "threshold" required by stakeholders.

- **Timeliness**. Timeliness means information is reported on a regular basis so stakeholders may make informed decisions. If information is delayed, for example, stakeholders may not be able to respond to the report. Consistent, regular reporting of information is desirable.

- **Clarity**. The guidelines emphasize how information must be available, understandable, and accessible to stakeholders using the report. Highly technical financial information may not be understandable. New packaging or a product design may be understandable to a trained engineer but not to a stakeholder without such training. The language in a report must be clear and at the level of education of an average reader.

- **Reliability**. When stakeholders read the sustainability report of a company, they want to know how reliable it is. They want to be able to examine the quality of the information and establish its materiality. Is the evidence available? Are documents accessible? When companies gather, record, compile, analyze, and disclose sustainable information and processes, stakeholders want to establish its veracity.

Reporting Guidance for Boundary Setting in Part 1. The last stage of Part 1 requires the organization to determine which entities' performance will be presented in the report. "Boundary setting" provides clarity to stakeholders and helps them understand what the report covers. It identifies areas of control and relationships among subsidiaries and joint ventures. Some entities within an organization may provide information at different intervals or their performance activities may occur in different degrees of impact. The degree of impact will be a key indicator for what content will be included in the report. Boundary setting is a necessary part of defining report content, quality, and boundary. The ultimate goal of Part 1 is transparency, accuracy, and completeness. If a company achieves these guidelines, it is ready to address the framework for reporting in Part 2, the quality of the report itself.

Part 2: Standard Disclosures

The GRI guidelines entitled Part 2 as "Standard Disclosures," which specifies the base content that should appear in a sustainability report. There are three categories of disclosures contained in the guidelines, Strategy and Profile, Management Approach, and Performance Indicators. Table 6.3 summarizes these categories and indicates brief examples in each category:

The GRI reporting guidelines for sustainability measure, disclose, and account for organizational performance. Most organizations are working toward sustainable development and the GRI guidelines provide an objective framework for the organization to achieve its objective. The sustainability report follows the measuring, disclosing, and accounting,

Table 6.3. Standard Disclosures

Category	Explanation of category
Strategy and profile	Disclosures that set the overall context for understanding organizational performance such as its strategy, profile, and governance. Examples: • Strategy and analysis (mission, vision, key impacts, risks, and opportunities), organizational profile (name, primary brands, products, services, structure, location, scale), parameters of the report itself (report profile, scope, and boundary), GRI Content Index, governance including commitments and engagement.
Management approach	Disclosures that cover how an organization addresses a given set of topics in order to provide context for understanding performance in a specific area. This category establishes the next level of detail of the organization's approach to managing the sustainability topics associated with risks and opportunities. • Economic performance • Market presence • Indirect economic impacts
Performance indicators	Disclosures that elicit comparable information on the economic, environmental, and social performance indicators of the organization. • *economic* indicators include economic performance, market presence, and indirect economic impacts • *environmental* indicators include materials used, energy consumption, water withdrawal and sources, biodiversity, and emissions (counting effluents and waste), products and services, compliance, and transportation • *social* indicators include four aspects: (a) labor practices and decent work (employment, labor and management relations, occupational health and safety, training and education, diversity and equal opportunity, equal remuneration for men and women), (b) human rights (investment and procurement practices, nondiscrimination, freedom of association and collective bargaining, child labor, forced and compulsory labor, security practices, indigenous rights, assessment, and remediation), (c) society–(local communities, corruption, public policy, anticompetitive behavior, and compliance, and (d) product responsibility (customer health and safety, product and service labeling, marketing communications, customer privacy, compliance).

Source: Adapted from GRI sustainability reporting guidelines.

and is a mechanism for transparency. The report requires companies to be accountable, promotes openness and trust, and cause participation and collaboration with stakeholders. GRI guidelines emphasize that the report should be a balanced and reasonable representation of the sustainability performance. Remember, the goal is transparency.

Good Reporting Practices

We close with a summary of recommended communication practices introduced by James Margolis and Mindy Gomes Casseres in an article posted on Greenbiz.com.[21] They work as partner and consultant, respectively, with Environmental Resources Management, a consulting company based in the UK. Their article reported on a workshop with 20 of the world's leading companies who discussed strategies in sustainability reporting. We select four strategies to present here. In the top 10 list, the first strategy focused on *materiality*. Material topics must first be determined before the report can be written, a point we made earlier in our discussion on GRI guidelines.

The next strategy that emerged from the workshop suggested the report should *resonate* or show the personality of the company. Such uniqueness can be done in several ways. When corporations assign writers to compile the report, they are given the task to capture a reflection of the culture of the company. The first goal of course is to accurately reflect sustainability performance, but the writers seek to present the information in a unique, interesting way to stakeholders. Report writers, for example, may tell unique stories that describe people involved in a social activity. The story may be about improved education of children, enhanced health of a community, or contributions to a cause for less fortunate individuals. These stories focus on individuals and typically show faces embedded within the story. Storytelling is effective and can be used to reflect personality and resonate with stakeholders.

Besides managing multiple audiences, knowing your data, and investing carefully in technology, the companies also recommended working effectively with internal and external partners. This point cannot be over stated. We stressed in Chapter 2 the importance of engagement with stakeholders and balanced communication. Sustainability reports must be adapted to the stakeholder audience. "Working effectively" may mean joint planning and strategy sessions with internal and external partners. The engagement process will be crucial to effective sustainability reporting.

Finally, we reiterate one last suggested strategy from the workshop. The seventh on the top 10 list stated, "To Integrate or Not to Integrate" referring to decision to combine the annual company report with the annual sustainability report. We mentioned in earlier examples how the Clorox Company and the Munich Airport had combined economic, environmental, citizenship, and social responsibility factors into one report. This integrated sustainability reporting works well for many companies, and we recommend considering it closely.

Put Into Practice!

Review the different Reporting Principles and Guidance in Table 6.2. Assess your own company's reporting practices according to each of the four principles from Part 1. Review the definitions first and write your assessment in the second column.

Reporting principle	Assessment of your company's reporting practices:
1. Materiality	
2. Stakeholder inclusiveness	
3. Sustainability context	
4. Completeness	

Summary

The reporting standards presented in this chapter, especially the GRI guidelines, provide your company with a benchmark procedure for sustainability reporting. Once you have "made the leap" into standardized reporting of sustainability performance, your company will connect and communicate with stakeholders in an important way. They will realize your communication efforts about sustainability are for real and they will begin to measure your company's performance by objective standards. The GRI guidelines are not just another reporting procedure to add to your list. The guidelines provide ways for your company's sustainability performance to be measured and to be made available for stakeholders to see.

CHAPTER 7

Cause-Related Marketing & Social Marketing

Green and sustainability marketing present unique challenges, not the least of which is the lack of standards for determining what it means to be a green and sustainable product—or a green company[1]

Sustainability marketing has emerged as a growing megatrend today among small, medium, and large businesses. We have seen the rapid evolution of traditional marketing approaches to be inclusive of sustainability. New marketing concepts address ecological issues such as "green" or environmental causes and social issues. These sustainability causes and activities exist to some degree in most businesses and organizations today. According to Belz and Peattie,[2] sustainability marketing is a broad category of marketing that purposes to do two things. First, it accepts the limitations of traditional marketing, which is directed toward increased consumerism and, second, it suggests true sustainable development can only be achieved by active involvement at the corporate level or by government intervention.

Sustainability marketing recognizes how the "pull" and "push" of traditional marketing encourages customers to increase consumption of products and services. Consumers are told, "buy more, consume more, update or upgrade your product even if it is not necessary." To move consumers toward a more sustainable lifestyle, we believe businesses must change fundamentally to reach true sustainable development.

We begin the chapter with a review of the traditional "marketing mix," including the 4 Ps, and provide sustainability examples related to each part of the mix. In the next sections we narrow our focus to two tools currently in use and growing in popularity: cause-related marketing (CRM) and social marketing. We present state-of-the-art definitions, discuss concepts, and describe applications in each of these CSR marketing areas. CRM is part of the overall marketing mix, and we describe ways this important area can be communicated effectively. In the final section, we examine social marketing, differentiating it from CRM, and describe ways social marketing is communicated effectively.

Innocent smoothies. This company will be introduced again in the next chapter, but we examine it here from a marketing perspective. The company is a UK business that has the interesting name of "Innocent" smoothies. It was begun in 1999 in London by three Cambridge University graduates developing a smoothie drink and selling it at a music festival. The three entrepreneurs had placed a large sign at the festival, asking attendees if they thought they should give up their jobs and make smoothies. Two bins were placed in front of the sign, one labeled "yes" and the other labeled "no." People voted by dropping their empty container in the appropriate bin. By the end of the day the "yes" bin was full. The three men quit their jobs and began Innocent, a business that currently dominates the smoothie market in the UK. According to information on its website,[3] the company sells "over two million pure fruit smoothies each week in 11,000 outlets" and employs over 250 people who work across Europe. The business offers a variety of health drinks and juice products in 13 different countries, totaling revenues in excess of £100 million each year.

Innocent also developed a creative marketing approach to children in its packaging of smoothies. A YouTube clip explains how kids can receive a free package of basil, tomato, cress, carrot, sunflower, or violet seeds with Innocent

Company: Innocent

Industry: Beverages

Tool: Sustainability marketing

Lesson: Innocent gives an excellent illustration of social marketing in changing children's behavior by planting trees. The company uses effectively eco-labels and branding to build its product. Creative marketing illustrates how the economic and social bottom lines are both improved.

(Continued)

Kids smoothies and Innocent Fruit Tube products. After enjoying the smoothie or fruit, children may use the carton to add soil, plant the seeds, and add water. Parents are also provided information on the website about the safe contents of the products.[4]

Innocent makes use of eco-labeling and sustainability marketing. Eco-labeling is marketing or identification of a product by appropriately labeling its source contents on the package. Innocent ensures that all of its bananas come from Rainforest Alliance accredited farms, using the alliance's eco-label on its packaging. Innocent also uses 100 percent Forest Stewardship Council certified material for kids products and adult smoothie cartons, applying the FSC eco-label to its products. The company clearly brands its sustainability efforts and communicates well its sustainable development through eco-labels.

Innocent illustrates how a company can be creative in product packaging that also has enhance sustainability. Communication on the company website includes a number of ways Innocent measures the carbon impact of its juice packs and reduces the carbon footprint:[5]

- Use less: as little material as possible per pack
- Don't use up new stuff: go for as much recycled and/or renewable material as possible
- Close the loop: use materials and pack formats that are easy to recycle
- Lower its impact: deliberately avoid high carbon materials follows developed sustainable standards for packaging

The Marketing Mix in Responsible Business

Mainstream marketing concepts traditionally focus on the 4 Ps, product (or service), price, place (or distribution), and promotion which can be applied on the responsible business context as illustrated in Figure 7.1. Each part of the marketing mix applies to sustainability marketing when planning, conducting, and evaluating marketing campaigns. Weinreich[6] added other Ps to sustainability to be discussed later in the chapter.

The **product** typically refers to the physical merchandise a business manufactures and markets, but it is also a service a company offers.

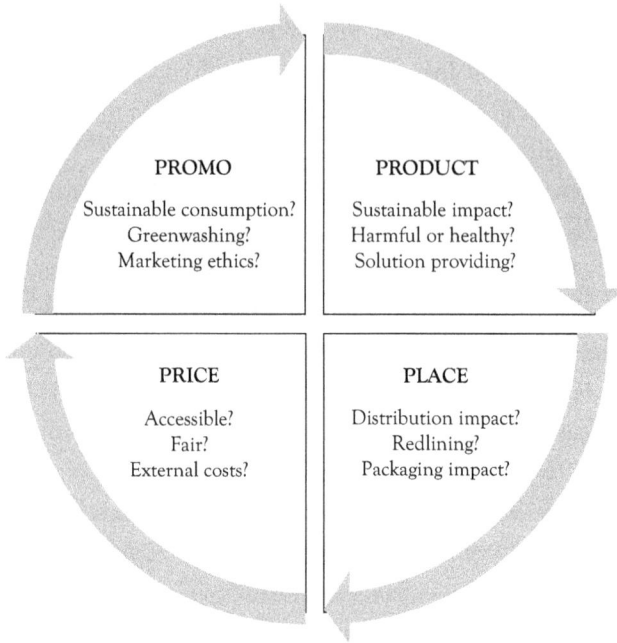

Figure 7.1. Exemplary responsible business considerations throughout the marketing mix.

Hotels and tour companies may exclusively market their services to select clientele interested in sustainable practices, promoting less water usage in towel or linen service, natural lighting, and organic coffees or foods served in the restaurants. Banking services, accounting services, maintenance services, or cleaning services for organizations represent growing areas of service marketing. Customers are interested in their reduced CO_2 footprint on the environment. Service marketing also dominates the health industry, where start-up companies have specialized in medical services for individuals confined to residences and for aging populations or individuals with unique medical needs. Sustainable, holistic treatments may be marketed to such individuals as part of a specialized service.

   Can a product be an idea? Starbucks thinks so. The company markets itself as a community of people gathered in their stores making conversation over a cup of coffee and enjoying free internet together, implying that the "idea" is a group people using their products in community.

In the product area of marketing, manufacturers and designers can lead the way by differentiating their merchandise with sustainable characteristics. Companies also can eliminate products with unacceptable socio-environmental performance. New product innovation may include features and characteristics which are sustainable. Similarly, service companies can reduce the environmental footprint of their services and the impact on the local environment. The ways products reflect sustainable development in a company are as various as the mission and vision statements of companies.

Price refers to what the customer will give in exchange for the manufactured product or service. In a broader sense, price may include the "cost of production, a signal of quality to consumers, a basis for market segmentation, a reflection of the demand that exists for a product ... and a key marketing variable that can be influenced to achieve a wide variety of marketing objectives."[7] Sustainability pricing involves all of these factors, especially if the brand image of the service or product allows the company to charge higher prices than normal. Starbucks, for instance, charges premium prices in large part because of their sustainable brand image.

Unusual pricing for sustainability... In 2009 Glaxo Smith Kline (GSK), a London-based pharmaceutical company, made a commitment to significantly reduce prices for patented medicines and vaccines in least developed countries (LDCs). Individuals at the bottom of the pyramid, primarily in East and West Africa, are offered medicines at GSK's manufacturing cost. The company's goal is to reduce prices to no more than 25% of their price in the UK or France.[8]

Another example illustrates unusual pricing for sustainability. The British Broadcast Company (BBC, 2011) reported that Reebok shoes will sell shoes for as little as $1 in India as a promotional vehicle. If so, the shoes would be one of the cheapest pairs of branded trainers anywhere. The idea was to create a "social business" that would help stimulate the local economy.

Sustainable pricing is handled in different ways. Some companies decide to transfer the cost of the company's environmental footprint to customers, giving them the option of paying a small amount above the actual cost of the product or service. The additional fee is small, typically, and it offsets the CO_2 impact. U.S.-based United Airlines, now a part of Continental Airlines, publishes information on its website to explain carbon offsetting, "the act of mitigating (offsetting) greenhouse gas emissions from human activities, including travel, which releases CO_2. When you offset your travel, your contribution goes to fund projects that are designed to reduce your calculated amount of personal CO_2 impact in the atmosphere."[6] The extra amount the customer pays is based on the length of travel. An overseas flight adds more CO_2 to the atmosphere than a short domestic flight, and the customer chooses which kind of program they want their money to benefit. Through this program, United Airlines emphasizes its commitment to promoting environmental responsibility within the culture of its company.

Other companies may choose to include the sustainability cost in the price of the product or service, causing an increase in the price to the customer. But few customers are willing to pay more for a sustainable product. When the price for a sustainable product is the same for an identical, non-sustainable product, then customers will choose sustainability. Manufacturers incorporate other methods of sustainable practices. Makers of laundry detergents, for instance, use less plastic resin in a container and offer the customer a larger-sized container containing more detergent but less packaging. As a result the customer buys more detergent at one time and receives a lower price per load of laundry. Thus, manufacturers are reducing the amount of packaging material, which costs less for the company and the customer and leaves a smaller carbon footprint, and providing a better buy for the consumer.

In traditional marketing, the third P, *place,* usually refers to transportation or distribution systems, or to the physical point of exchange between buyer and seller. Sustainability in transportation can be realized in lessened environment impact of distribution systems, and innovative companies may open new sustainable distribution channels that use less fossil fuel and have fewer CO_2 emissions. Consider one example. Sitting in our car in a left-turn lane while our engine idles may not be significant to most of us, but *The New York Times* magazine[10] reported how a small, efficient change in transportation routes by a large company can have a significant impact in reduced CO_2 emissions. Using sophisticated software, United Parcel Service (UPS) eliminated most left turns for its 95,000 package delivery trucks and reduced "28.5 million miles off its delivery routes, which has resulted in savings of roughly three million gallons of gas and has reduced CO_2 emissions by 31,000 metric tons."[11] UPS serves 220 countries and delivers nearly 16 million packages daily. The company reported $53 billion in revenue in 2011 and employs nearly 400,000 worldwide.[12] The small change made a large difference in the environment and increased the economic bottom line of UPS.

Developing sustainability in transportation systems is also realized by minimizing packaging designs of products and reducing weight and amount of required space. Laasch and Conaway[13] described sustainable development in PUMA, a German-based company doing business in over 120 countries and employing more than 9500 people worldwide.[14] The sports and athletic wear business launched a highly innovative new shoe package design in 2010. The classic shoe box and plastic bag were redesigned with 65 percent less cardboard and materials, but more importantly less packing means less shipping weight. Through packaging redesign, the company lessened its environmental impact and increased its economic bottom line.

Promotion is the fourth "P" of the marketing mix. It is often called marketing communication instead of promotion, and it includes all the messages exchanged between the seller and the ultimate consumer. The promotional mix elements represent both personal and nonpersonal communication. Personal messages include any communication that addresses the individual customer directly, such as personal selling. Other messages sent one-way to large groups of people are more nonpersonal, such as mass media advertising, websites, public relations, and publicity, unless the media channel is interactive with the customer. The sustainable characteristics of a product or service are often promoted directly to the customer. Customers are told if they buy a certain product, the proceeds help a certain group of people or a cause.

Sustainability communication is most clearly integrated throughout this P of marketing. The most significant change in promotion over the last decade, safely identified as radical innovation, is the shift to relationship-marketing communication. Customers become a part of the promotional process through the channel of interactive, online media. Now, individuals can comment on a product's characteristics online in a blog or web page. Businesses can dialog with customers over sustainable characteristics or improvement of packaging design. Creative customers with new ideas provide the company with an amazing resource of intellectual property.

A significant area of relational communication occurs when businesses dialog with stakeholders before developing new products or beginning sustainability initiatives. If a business will utilize feedback and incorporate ideas from key stakeholders, the success of new initiatives will have good chances of success. Before this communication can occur, marketing personnel and strategic planners must follow the normal process of setting objectives, developing one integrated message, selecting appropriate channels, and effectively communicating with stakeholders.

Cause-Related Marketing

We now focus on two specific management tools currently in use and which are growing in popularity, CRM and social marketing. **CRM** occurs when a company offers to contribute a specified amount of revenues from sales of its products or services to a dedicated cause.[15] CRM, not to be confused with customer relationship marketing, usually exists at the product level because a portion of the sales of that product are dedicated to a cause.

CRM differs from normal *cause* marketing. This distinction is important because of the connection between the product and the donation in CRM. Businesses that engage in normal cause marketing may operate a social foundation or charity, but the business does give a set portion of a product sale or service to the foundation. McDonald's engages in normal commercial marketing for a cause because it does not specify a set portion of its restaurant sales to the Ronald McDonald House charity. CRM would imply the existence of a direct connection. McDonald's, however, is the largest corporate donor to the charity, employees volunteer their participation, owners of McDonald's franchises are members of the charity's board, and donation boxes in McDonald's restaurants exist to fund the charity. The charity markets itself for the cause of health and well-being of children but does not engage in CRM.

CRM also differs from traditional commercial marketing, although both follow similar marketing principles. The purpose of each type distinguishes the two. Typically, commercial marketing purposes to benefit the organization conducting the marketing campaign. CRM seeks to benefit the cause and society. While the objective of commercial marketing may be increased sales and profit, the objective of CRM is directed toward sustainable development and involves a sustainable business activity.

Sustainable causes are varied and may involve people, organizations, or the environment. Atkins (1999) identified American Express as the first major business to pioneer a CRM campaign. The company donated a portion of funds received from credit card fees toward renovation of the Statute of Liberty on Liberty Island in New York. Today, American Express still gives a portion of funds received from new credit cards and credit card fees to the World Monuments Fund and the National Trust for Historic Preservation. Many types of CRM exist but we examine four primary types: (1) standard CRM, (2) noncash, (3) cause branding, and (4) multicause branding.

Types of CRM

Standard CRM is the type we have just described with American Express. The business donates a cash portion of every product or service sold to a cause. This marketing approach is popular today and used by small, medium, and large businesses. *Noncash* donations represent a second type of CRM and exist when companies give in-kind donations to a cause based on the quantity of goods sold of a certain product. TOMS shoes, discussed in detail in Chapter 1, donates a pair of shoes to a child in need for every pair sold, or a "One for One" campaign.[16]

Cause branding is a third approach to CRM. Different companies often will support the same cause. The cause may be global, operating in numerous countries, and may have its own eco-label or brand, which allows different businesses to connect certain products or entire product lines to the cause. Several examples illustrate this type of CRM. Product (RED) may be the most well-known global cause, which fights for an AIDS-free Africa by the year 2015. Product (RED) asks companies that adopt the colorful, unique RED label to give up some of its profits to fight AIDS. Converse Shoes "will contribute a portion of the profits from the purchase of every red-colored Chuck Taylor All Star shoe to the Global Fund to help eliminate AIDS."[17] Apple Computer makes a similar contribution. When customers purchase leather, red-colored Smart covers for their iPad2, Apple donates a portion of the sale to the Global Fund to eliminate AIDS. Nike, Starbucks, and Dell all participate in RED in similar fashion.

Cause branding is also illustrated by the pink ribbon symbol of the Susan B. Komen breast cancer cause. The foundation claims "the Susan G. Komen Race for the Cure Series is the world's largest and most successful education and fundraising event for breast cancer ever created."[18] In 2011 the cause organized 16 international races in 11 countries. A portion of the proceeds from each 5K or 10K race go to the foundation, and race participants ask friends to donate an additional $1 toward the cause. Finally, the recognizable face of actor Paul Newman's is placed on his product lines. Newman's Own, a food company founded in 1982 by the actor, donates all profits from its food products to charity. According to the company website, "over $300 million has been given to thousands of charities since 1982."[19] The company is a private, for profit business that operates in 15 countries. The amount contributed is based on the level of profit.

Other common types of CRM exist and may be popular in certain locations around the globe. **Multicause marketing** is an approach used by a company when it contributes a specified amount to a dedicated cause, similar to donations in the standard approach, yet the causes rotate over a period of time. A company, for example, may contribute the same percentage of sales or service each month or year and select a different cause for each subsequent contribution.

Put it to Practice!

Match the four primary types of cause-related branding we discussed in the preceding section. Write either (1) **standard** CRM, (2) **noncash**, (3) **cause branding**, or (4) **multicause** branding in the appropriate space on the right.

Definition	Type of CRM
A company contributes a specified amount to a dedicated cause, yet the cause rotates over a period of time	
A company gives in-kind donations to a cause based on the quantity of goods sold of a certain product	
A business donates a percentage of every product or service sold to a cause	
Different companies support the same cause, which may have its own eco-label or brand, and it allows the businesses to connect certain products or entire product lines to the cause	

Social Marketing

In contrast with CRM, *social marketing* purposes to change individuals' behavior to improve their well-being and that of society.[20] While CRM addresses the proportion of contributions from products and sales, social marketing markets to change an individual's behavior. Although similar marketing principles are employed in commercial marketing, social marketing differs in its purpose. Social marketing purposes to improve the well-being of individuals or society.

What kinds of business use social marketing? Any company may engage in social marketing that wishes to improve the health of its own employees, to benefit the welfare of citizens outside the company, or improve the environment or society in general. Most of us are familiar with public social marketing. Billboard advertising, television commercials, and social media constantly promote health issues related to obesity, physical activity, sexual issues, alcohol abuse, or smoking. Each of these public health campaigns urges us to change our behavior for the better. Other public campaigns are directed toward social problems such as the helping the poor, improving literacy rates, or reducing domestic violence in homes. Traditionally, government agencies, universities, or private foundations fund these promotions designed to benefit people and society.

The social marketing addressed in this chapter focuses on business instead of marketing by government agencies or public foundations. As more businesses use social marketing, innovative ideas emerge through the business sector to improve people's life styles. For example, Volkswagen's Fun Theory website illustrates an interesting type of social marketing. The company hosts a contest each year that awards the most innovative idea for changing people's behavior, emphasizing that fun is the easiest way to do so.[21] First place winners earn 2500 euros for their idea and assistance to actually make the idea happen. One winner promoted use of stairs instead of taking an escalator. The contest winners turned a set of public stairs into a piano keyboard. Those who went up and down stepped on piano keys and heard the piano tone through nearby speakers. Taking the stairs became fun and encouraged a significant increase in use over the nearby escalator. Another Fun Theory idea was directed toward recycling. The winner created a bottle bank arcade, a machine which looked like an arcade game and displayed points on an LCD display whenever someone dropped a plastic bottle or aluminum can into the machine. Placed on a sidewalk in a city area in Europe, the idea was to make it fun for someone to recycle. Results showed over 100 people used the bottle bank arcade in one evening while a conventional bottle bank nearby was used only twice in the same period. Such innovative ideas in sustainability marketing help promote the well-being of people and encourage healthy life styles.

Procter & Gamble (P&G), generally well known as a responsible company, illustrates another good example of social marketing. In its 2008 Corporate Sustainability Report, the company established five sustainability strategies, one of which purposed to "improve children's lives through P&G's social responsibility programs."[22] Children are helped through the building of schools in Asia and tens of thousands of children have better education facilities. To improve the lives of children, safe drinking water, nutrition, and hygiene programs have been provided. P&G shows how social marketing involves much more than simply creating awareness of a need and proving resources to improve the well-being of children. Behavior change through social marketing involves several steps, which we discuss in the following section.

One of the most important aspects of effective communication through social marketing "involves understanding the response process the receiver may go through in moving toward a specific behavior," such as purchasing a product.[23] Theories of behavior change abound and marketers have studied how to get consumers to respond to a campaign. To move someone from initial awareness to actually changing a behavior involves multistep processes which are illustrated in Figure 7.2. Most theories include the following stages, which may not be sequential and may occur over a period of time. Some behavior change includes a latency effect, where learning and change take place cognitively, but the actual behavior occurs at a later date.[24]

Awareness or attention. Social marketing first draws attention to or creates awareness of the social cause. This stage is primarily at the cognitive level for the consumer. Previously, individuals may have had no awareness or knowledge about the cause. Thus, P&G first must create awareness about the significant number of children in India that lack sufficient education. Sustainability reports, press releases, or

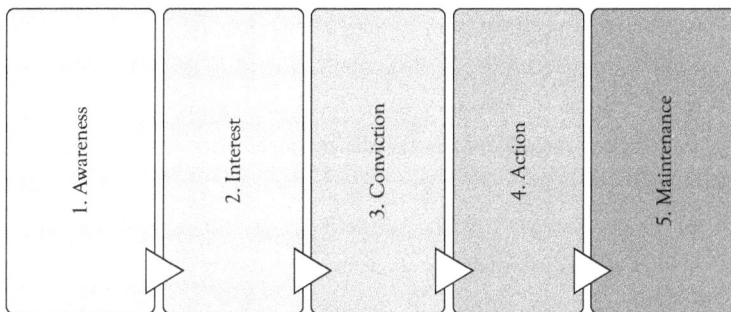

1. Awareness   2. Interest   3. Conviction   4. Action   5. Maintenance

Figure 7.2. Stages of the social marketing process.

information on product packaging may help create this awareness and disseminate information. When consumers become aware of the cause and their knowledge or comprehension grows, they will proceed to the next stage.

1. *Interest or liking.* This step represents a move from cognitive awareness to an affective or emotional stage. The consumer begins *feeling* something about the cause. This stage often involves developing a favorable preference for the specific cause over other similar causes, and it is also a "yielding" stage emotionally where the individual develops participation at a minimal level. Perhaps a customer of P&G will begin researching children's education in India after becoming aware of the extent of the issue, not just to verify P&G's statistics, but to learn more about the issue.

2. *Conviction.* Once an individual develops a liking for the cause, conviction develops and a decision is made to take action. The decision is for the future and may be low-level or high-level involvement. The convinced individual may decide to purchase products that P&G has advertised, supporting the cause of children's education. Or a direct financial donation may be given that is more substantial than the purchase of a product. The action or behavior has not yet happened and may be thwarted depending on how circumstances change.

3. *Action.* Finally, the individual moves from the feeling stage and takes action. Awareness of the cause first was created, interest or liking in the cause was developed, conviction occurred, and action was taken. The consumer purchased the product, a new lifestyle was adopted, or a change in behavior occurred. The process to move from awareness to action is complex and social marketers must understand the different stages before a successful campaign can be completed.

4. *Maintenance.* Many social marketing experts include a fifth stage of behavior change labeled maintenance.[25] In this stage the individual continues to be involved in the cause. Once individuals reach the maintenance stage, they may support the cause over time, participate or become involved, or even may develop a lifestyle of sustainability.

Put it to Practice!

Match the stages of behavior change mentioned in the list by writing the correct stage in the blank on the right.

Description of behavior change stage	Name of stage
The feeling stage where the consumer has developed a favorable preference for the specific cause over other similar causes.	
The stage where the consumer purchased the product, adopted a new lifestyle, or changed a particular behavior.	
The stage where the individual continues to be involved in the cause.	
The cognitive stage that first draws attention to or creates awareness of the cause.	
The feeling stage where the behavior has not yet happened but the consumer has decided to take action in the future.	

LOHAS lifestyles. A large market segment of individuals have reached Stage 5, Maintenance, after changing their behavior toward sustainability. They are maintaining a continuous lifestyle of healthy living. The segment is identified as "Lifestyles of Health and Sustainability" (LOHAS). LOHAS represents "an estimated $290 billion U.S. marketplace for goods and services focused on health, the environment, social justice, personal development, and sustainable living."[26] The organization's website estimates 13–19 percent of the U.S. adults identify themselves as LOHAS consumers and other research shows one in four adult Americans is part of this group. The typical LOHAS consumer would be attracted to organic products and green buildings that include energy saving appliances, sustainable flooring, or renewable energy systems. LOHAS tourists prefer eco-tourism travel or adventures. These customers prefer natural lifestyles and alternative transportation. Companies cannot ignore this market segment that is estimated at $290 billion annually in the U.S and growing.

Put in to Practice!

Use the worksheet in the following table to analyze one communication activity of your company by first analyzing it verbally and then scoring it. Conclude by thinking about potential activities for improvement.

Company task	Activity analysis	Score (+,=,–)
(A) My company's marketing mix communicates sustainability objectives throughout products, price, place, and promotion.		
(B) My company's has engaged in CRM or has the potential to successfully engage in CRM		
(C) My company's has engaged in social marketing or has the potential to successfully use this marketing tool.		
(D) My company has an excellent understanding of the stages of behavior change in social marketing.		

Overall Score (Minimum –4, maximum +4).

Summary

Effective marketing communication lies at the heart of a company's efforts to successfully engage in sustainability activities. The progress a company makes toward becoming a sustainable business relies on effective communication through marketing.

We focused on two specific marketing management tools identified as CRM and social marketing. Cause-marketing occurs when your company offers to contribute a specified amount of revenues to a dedicated cause. Social marketing, which purposes to change individuals' behavior to improve their well-being and influence society, is a popular tool of marketing in business as well as government and public foundations. We hope you will consider one of these two tools in your own business. Our focus centered on business examples, such as Volkswagen's Fun Theory contest. Moving consumers to the action and maintenance requires a sophisticated understanding of the behavioral change process.

CHAPTER 8

Nonverbal Stakeholder Communication

Actions speak louder than words, but not nearly as often. Don't say the old lady screamed. Bring her on and let her scream.

—Mark Twain

A common belief is that communication is only about words and talk. Nevertheless, when saying no words at all, one cannot avoid communicating. Nonverbal communication conveys more meaning in social conversation than the words themselves.[1] In this chapter we focus on nonverbal communication through the design of the company's responsible business activities. We will use two examples to illustrate the effect of nonverbal communication design on stakeholders, the UK-based fruit smoothie maker Innocent and the Japanese car manufacturer Toyota. Such nonverbal communication design through responsible business has the potential to achieve positive outcomes, often even more effectively than direct communication activities.

Will a good product sell itself without a big marketing effort? When Toyota launched the first mass-produced hybrid car Prius in 1997, the marketing budget was very restricted. The logical consequence was to focus on the Prius's attractiveness as the first auto industry alternative for the grassroots

Company:	Toyota Motors
Industry:	Automobile
Tool:	Design & Positioning
Lesson: A differentiated sustainable innovation product, meeting untapped market demand, providing a positive socio-environmental impact and emotional attachment is almost "self-communicating."	

(Continued)

(*Continued*)

groups of environmentally conscious customers. These groups turned into product evangelists who actively promoted the Prius "in-the-scene" from mouth-to-mouth.[2] With the US market launch in 2000, Hollywood celebrities discovered the Prius in masses and triggered a marketing buzz when paparazzi regularly snapped and published celebrity pictures of superstars next to their hybrid. An estimate is that at least 70 top-tier Hollywood celebrities, including Harrison Ford, Cameron Diaz, and Tom Hanks, owned and displayed their hybrids.[3] Once fuel prices rose, the fuel efficient characteristics made hybrid cars a logical choice. The Prius was successfully pole-positioned among product alternatives and without much additional marketing effort, first for owners of car fleets and then for a broader public.[4] In 2007, the Prius became the bestselling hybrid car, not because of exceptional direct marketing and communication efforts, but because of the car's distinct body design. Unlike with other hybrids, which were hardly distinguishable from nonhybrid cars, people knew that the Prius was an environmental friendly car when they saw it, and Prius owners enjoyed sending this clear nonverbal message.[5]

While Toyota's focus achieved strong nonverbal communication through the product design, the company Innocent also excels in its nonverbal communication by taking a more holistic approach going far beyond the mere product.

From its humble beginning in a small stall at a local Jazz festival, the British fruit smoothie company Innocent has grown to a multinational company with more than US$ 150 million revenues. A sign next to that humble fruit stand asked for a vote: "Should we quit our jobs to make those smoothies?"

Company:	Innocent
Industry:	Beverages
Tool:	Congruence

Lesson: Congruently implementing responsible business practices throughout all processes, products, the supply chain and the company's broader sphere of influence sends a strong and credible message simultaneously to a broad set of stakeholders. The stronger the responsibility message, the easier it is to be destroyed through incongruent actions.

(*Continued*)

The answer was "yes." Innocent reinforces the company motto of innocence through implementation of responsible practices in all parts of its activity, from sourcing (sustainable and fair) to production (eco-efficient operations programs), to products (purely natural-no additives).[6] For a company calling itself Innocent, any other strategy would endanger the overall credibility. Does it sound too good to be true? It is. In 2009 the company accepted an offer by the Coca Cola Company to buy shares, which resulted in a dramatic rebound-effect. Consumers were shocked, started counter-campaigning, and even boycotting the company.[7] Had Innocent lost its innocence?

Verbal versus Nonverbal Communication and the Creation of Synergies

Companies, as people, communicate verbally and nonverbally. The message received through **nonverbal communication** includes physical characteristics of the communicator or environmental surroundings of the verbal communication process. Business communication often has a strong focus on the easier to control verbal communication part. However, stakeholders of companies interpret verbal communication through a whole world of nonverbal cues, which positively or negatively interact with the verbal message. A company effectively communicating responsible business has to excel in both verbal and nonverbal communication to ensure the communication goals can be achieved.

Innocent was able to nonverbally communicate their message of innocence and responsibility to consumers through its logo (a simplistic apple with a halo) and the purely natural quality of its product. The company communicated to employees through fun, humane working conditions; to suppliers, through fair trade practices; and to investors through the annual general meeting (AGM), which was conducted in an unusual, open, personal, and experiential style. Innocent calls the AGM "A Grown-up Meeting." Similarly, Toyota did not need words to claim environmental leadership when they launched the Prius as a first alternative to cars that had environmentally harmful traditional combustion engines.

An important part of nonverbal communication is the role of the communicative **environment** or context. In the case of Toyota the message "buy environmental friendly cars" found great resonance among stakeholders, as it was in line with cues in the broader environment. Customers increasingly showed environmental consciousness as gasoline prices were constantly increasing. Celebrities became aware of their role-model position and used the Prius as a tool to communicate their own environmentalist attitudes. The degree to which nonverbal communication favors or impedes companies' communication goals is directly connected to how receptive the stakeholder environment is for the message. Interestingly, the Prius itself became the source of the message. Stakeholders tended to receive and positively interpret messages about the Prius' environmentally friendly features and image.

Designing a responsible business that sends the right nonverbal messages is critical to the fulfillment of set communication purposes. As described in Figure 8.1, a bad design might create **dissynergies** between verbal and nonverbal communication, resulting in latent distrust, open criticism, tangible counter-activism against the company, or even complete boycotts. An excellent example for such dissynergy is the reaction to BP's renewed slogan beyond petroleum (verbal communication), which was not in accordance with the company's almost purely petroleum-based operations (nonverbal communication). Reactions included disbelief by the general public and sarcastic, aggressive online videos about the company.[8]

On the other hand, companies achieving a congruent relationship between verbal and nonverbal communication in responsible business are very likely to gain a broad number of **synergies** resulting

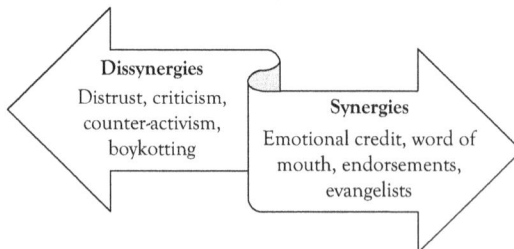

Figure 8.1. Synergies and dissynergies between responsible business design and communication.

in advantages. Stakeholders will give the company a certain emotional credit, which might lead to positive word of mouth, to active endorsements, or even to company "evangelists" who are fans of the responsible business and serve as voluntary brand ambassadors. In the case of TOMS Shoes (see Chapter 1), the company's one-for-one shoe donation business model wowed the press and started the spread of the message that resulted in the company running out of stock even before they had started marketing.[9]

The overarching goal of designing synergetic, verbal, and nonverbal communication systems must be to actively create positive synergies, such as in the case of TOMS. In contrast, the company wants to avoid dissynergies as observed in the case of BP. Figure 8.1 provides a simple model of four-elements for the creation of positive synergies when communicating responsible business. A company has to make sure it creates congruence throughout all verbal and nonverbal messages and makes the message distinct and emotive to create impressive real-life impacts.

Congruence, impact, distinctiveness, and emotiveness contribute to the creation of positive synergies. The more mutually reinforcing relationships are forged among the communicative factors, the more likely it is for the company to create **communication buzz**, also called "viral" or mouth-to-mouth communication, where the message is almost self-communicating, and therefore requires only little direct communication efforts.[10] It is important to note that a communication buzz may be either negative or positive. Strong dissynergies may lead to a negative communication buzz, leading to a situation where the company is harmed in its reputation.

Design Features for Successful Nonverbal Communication

Nonverbal responsible business communication in practice is about how your company has performed, what it is doing, and how it will relate to its environment. In the following section we will provide a basic framework for designing a nonverbal responsible business message for single activities or for the whole company, which is illustrated in Figure 8.2.

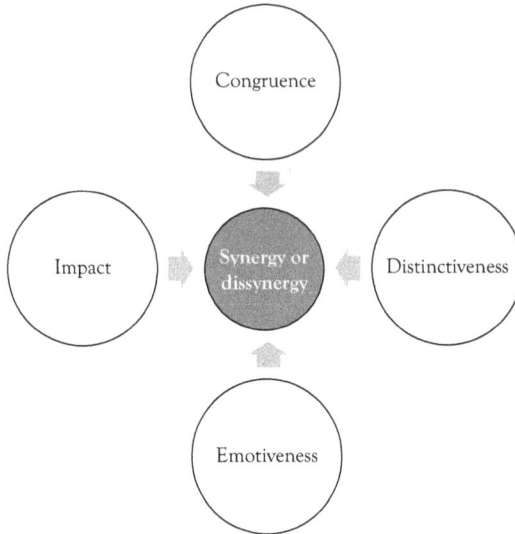

Figure 8.2. Synergetic design features for responsible business and communication.

These four design features applied jointly aim at the creation of synergies and the achievement of the desired communication buzz.

1. Creating **congruence** is of central importance in responsible business communication. Incongruence between a company's verbal and nonverbal communication easily destroy value. Congruence means matching the different types of verbal communication and all activities of the company throughout its sphere of influence. We will now focus on four exemplary areas of the company's sphere of influence: the supply chain, company processes, the products, and the broader company environment. The **supply chain** of a product runs from extraction of the first raw material to the product's use by the last consumer and is full of potential contradictions to the responsible business message companies send. Typical problems occur from bad labor practices by suppliers or licensing partners, environmental issues caused by suppliers' operations, and health or safety problems of products because of bad inputs delivered by suppliers. Sales practices of independent distributors may cause problems, or your **product** might send contradictory messages.

The company, Statoil, ranked first in Fortune's 2011 most responsible companies list, yet it was challenged by the company's main product petroleum's negative environmental characteristics.[11] Congruence with the company's general **environment** and broad tendencies helped Toyota in promoting the Prius, fueled by climate fears and rising oil prices. Also a company's **history and values** must be incongruent with the company's communication efforts. After the movie *The High Cost of Low Price*,[12] which criticized Walmart's as an irresponsible company, it would have been difficult for the company to credibly communicate itself as a responsibility leader.

Is congruence child's play? Lego, a company best known for its construction toys of interlocking plastic blocks, has achieved an impressive congruence between verbal communication on responsible business and nonverbal communication factors. Lego's main responsible business activities are centered on the themes of child development, education and family, all of which are well aligned with the company's main product. Lego's main stakeholder group is children, who are mainly addressed through messages to their parents. Their main stakeholder engagement platform online is titled "parents."[13] Lego also displays congruence with its founding values and history of not producing war-related sets. The company's founding father Ole Kirk Christiansen had made clear that he did not consider war child's play. In fact, Lego produces a few war-related sets. The company explains these sets congruently by the importance of conflict role play in normal healthy child development.[14]

In 2011 the company found itself involved in a supply-chain scandal, when being mentioned as one of the multinational companies producing goods for the coming Christmas sales in a Chinese company under sweatshop conditions.[15] Lego was able to communicate in the difficult situation congruently by stating how seriously the company takes supply-chain issues. Lego communicated that it had taken extensive precautions and would implement decisive actions.

(Continued)

(*Continued*)

The company did so despite not being the contracting company, but a licensing partner.[16] Congruence also involves attention to detail, especially in times of crisis.

Lego was able to capitalize on its congruent messages and positive impressions. A simple Google˚ search provides anecdotal evidence about Lego's congruence in communicating responsible business. Searching with the terms "Lego" and "trouble" does not gives a single result on the first search page that would question the company's responsible business performance.

A Google search for Disney and social responsibility reveals a very different picture. Despite Disney being an acknowledged leader in responsible business,[17] seven out of ten Google hits address the company's irresponsibility. The negative coverage ranges from criticism of the company's CEO's performance and reputation,[18] to toys with choking hazards.[19] Several criticisms address the values implied in Disney's flagship characters, the princesses[20] and Bambi.[21] In the case of Lego, stakeholders seem to be enthusiastic about the company as can be seen in the Lego Ambassador program, through which 70 volunteers from 30 countries actively promote the company in the community.[22]

2. Making a **positive impact** is a necessary precondition to creating self-reinforcing word of mouth. Some companies commit the mistake of talking about their impact even before it is created and assured. Communicating performance should not be confused with communicating activity. For instance, a company that tries to impress through planting 10,000 trees (activity) in a reforestation campaign, would be well-advised to wait with their communication activities until those trees have survived the first year (impact). Communicating positive impact with the goal of creating word of mouth requires shaping simple, but powerful messages that are easy to be passed on. Such a message can often be created involving concise numbers.

   There are many good examples of companies successfully communicating positive impact: The movie theater chain Cinépolis communicates that they save 3000 eyes annually in their anticataract campaign.[23] TOMS shoes surprised stakeholders with their one millionth pair of shoes donated.[24] Pepsico with its "refresh everything" program has reached impressive numbers. Pepsi communicated it has engaged 79,000 volunteers and has improved 1.4 million lives.[25]

Nevertheless, the company has not created a communication buzz as strong as other companies. Why is that so? One reason might be language characteristics of the message. Stakeholders will ask themselves, "What did those volunteers do?" (activity versus performance) and "What does changing a life mean?" (complexity of message).

3. The **distinctiveness** of responsible business activities can be a powerful nonverbal communication tool. The more impressed stakeholders are about what you are doing, the more likely it is for them to spread the word. People were impressed, for example, about the possibility of a mass-produced hybrid car when Toyota started communicating about the Prius. One powerful outcome was the extensive celebrity endorsement. TOMS shoes' buy-one, donate-one business model had never been seen before. The company turned into a "responsibility superstar" without much active communication effort. Ben and Jerry's cause-brands identify the company's ice cream with unique and often even controversial names. An example is the company's fair trade flavor is Coconutterly Fair.[26] Another "must-tell" is the promotional products company Earthimprint's biodegradable pen made of corn, which includes a seed. When the pen is empty, put it into the right spot of soil and create a new plant.[27]

4. It is not a new idea that **emotions** sell. Emotiveness of activities and messages is big plus when it comes to engaging stakeholders. For instance the Danone cause-related marketing campaign raised funds for the treatment of children with cancer and was powered by a series of highly emotional TV spots. The spots aimed to persuade viewers to identify with parents who have a child with cancer.[28] Social, environmental, and ethical topics have the potential to create strong emotions among stakeholders. Emotiveness in responsible business may be a two-sided sword. While positive emotions may be create through verbal communication, a company's nonverbal communication may create negative emotions beyond the business's control.

Table 8.1. Scoring the Quality of Responsible Communication Design for Exemplary Cases[1]

Company	Activity	Congruence	Impact	Distinctiveness	Emotiveness	Results
Toyota	Prius	(+) With environmental conditions, and with environmental practices in production.	(+) Paved the way to large scale production of CO_2-reduced cars.	(+) One of the first cars as an alternative to traditional combustion engine cars.	(=) At the beginning only emotive topic for environmentalists; later for broad public because of the climate change fear.	+3 → Positive marketing buzz and minimal communication efforts necessary.
Innocent	Company structuring	(=) High throughout business functions; low in the collaboration with Coca Cola	(+) Health promotion through product; fair trade and ecological agriculture	(+) High through search of highest social and environmental responsibility throughout all activities.	(=) High, through unique marketing communication and company history; intermediate, as there is no additional emotive cause involved at the core.	+2 → High for-free media coverage and enthusiasm about the company's business model, but strong negative reactions about the participation of The Coca Cola Company.
LEGO	Company reputation building	(+) High, through cause of child development, alignment with corporate values and history.	(=) Focuses on doing nothing wrong, but lacks activities with strong positive impact.	(−) Lacks strong differentiator in responsible business activities.	(+) Many stakeholders are enthusiastic about the Lego toys, because of the experience made as kids or with their own kids, which translates to Lego's emotive potential.	+1 → Little distinction through proactive responsible business activities, but excellent enthusiasm about product; Lego ambassador program as product evangelists

Pepsico	Refresh project	(–) Apart from the refresh slogan, the donations are hardly aligned with the company's core business.	(+) The impact of the project in total numbers is enormous, but they lack	(–) The only differentiation given is to brand it as the "refresh project." Apart from this detail, it looks like the donations, given by many other corporate foundations.	(+) Single projects supported through the program have high emotive potential, but the overall program does not send an integrated emotive message.	–1 → Costly campaign, with great impact, underperforming in its communicative potential.
BP	Slogan "Beyond Petroleum"	(–) Incongruence with petroleum-centered core business and BP's company name.	(–) Negative direct and indirect environmental impact of petroleum companies.	(–) No differentiation from other company slogans.	(–) Negatively emotive, because stakeholders perceived the slogan as greenwashing	–4 → Massive damage to brand instead of an aspired shift toward positive stakeholder perception.

[1] The scoring scheme works as follows: (–) signals a low score, (=) an intermediate score, and (+) a positive score.

As described in Table 8.1, all four categories of congruence, impact, distinctiveness, and emotiveness interact to create a communication design that facilitates synergies between verbal and nonverbal communication. The four factors aim at creating an overall message that "communicates itself." This communication design works as a system. Marketing communication for the Toyota Prius did not require marketing communication efforts as extensive as other in product launches. The nonverbal communication design was well done as was seen in the preceding examples. The car was **congruent** with general environmental conditions. Its **impact** as the first mass-produced alternative-engine vehicle was impressive. The **distinctiveness** from traditional internal combustion engines was overwhelming. The **emotiveness** was high, especially once climate change became a mainstream topic people were concerned about.

BP experienced the opposite situation. While verbal communication efforts were well-designed (logo, slogan, clips, etc.), nonverbal communication proved highly incongruent with the verbal and destroyed the company's reputation. The slogan "beyond petroleum" was not **congruent** with the company's core business that was far from being beyond petroleum. The overall environmental **impact** of any company in the petroleum business is perceived to be as negative. People often associate those companies with oil spills off-shore, global warming, and the destruction of ecosystems through onshore operations. The campaign was lacking **distinctiveness**, and was perceived as just another corporate branding effort. For stakeholders, the BP branding effort was negatively emotive, as stakeholders felt themselves taken as a fool (How can a company called BP be beyond petroleum?) and manipulated (Does BP want to make us believe that they are green while they are not?) by the company.

Put it to practice!

Use the worksheet in Table 8.2 to analyze one communication activity of your organization by first analyzing it verbally, then scoring it, and finally thinking about potential activities for improvement. Use *Table 8.2.* as orientation.

Table 8.2. Checklist Synergies Design and Communication

Company task	Activity analysis	Score (+,=,-)
(A) **Congruence**: My company has achieved congruence between communication and responsible business conducts, including supply chain, business environment, processes, and products.		
(B) **Emotiveness**: My company's responsible business conduct has the potential to evoke strong positive feelings, such as sympathy, personal attachment or even passion.		
(C) **Distinctiveness**: My company's responsible business conduct is unique or at least highly distinct from peers' activities.		
(D) **Impact**: My company's activities are characterized by positive impacts in the social, environmental and economic spheres.		

Overall Score (minimum −4; maximum +4).

Summary

Communicating in responsible business depends strongly on the verbal and nonverbal communication activities of companies. Nevertheless, nonverbal communication plays a powerful role in reaching communication goals in responsible business. We have examined a nonverbal communication model centered on the four good practices of congruence, impact, distinctiveness, and emotiveness. If a company excels in all four, it has the prerequisites to create strong synergies between verbal and nonverbal communication activities. Such synergies can lead to communication buzz, where the message about responsible business conducts "communicates itself" among stakeholders.

CHAPTER 9

Stakeholder Communication Online

The world's most sustainable companies fall short in communicating corporate social responsibility (CSR) on the internet ... many are locked in a once-a-year reporting mentality, failing to keep stakeholders updated in an engaging, dynamic, and ongoing manner. Above all, corporations aren't keeping pace with the needs of a skeptical audience for dialogue and engagement on the internet—from setting up effective feedback channels to adopting social media.[1]

"The internet is the future" is a commonplace saying, but what exactly does it mean? By 2012 we were connected with most of our friends (and strangers) worldwide on Facebook. We "twittered" and used mobile devices to access the internet from virtually everywhere. Those realities are normal nowadays, but imagine you could go back in time to 15 years ago and talk to a less connected version of yourself (the one who had just bought a banana-sized mobile phone). How would you be able explain to someone from the past that you can today share news with your 500 Facebook friends or 5000 Twitter followers from anywhere around the world in an instant? And the incredible changes that have taken place from 1995 to 2010 will likely be equaled, or even surpassed in the next five years.

A recent meta-study comparing the web in 2010 with an estimate in 2015 includes some interesting facts and predictions. In 2010 there were 2 billion internet users, 500 Million Facebook users, 150 million Twitter users, and 470 million smart phone devices. People spent 16 percent of their time online in social networks, 9.2 percent with instant messaging, 6.6 percent writing e-mails, and another 6.2 percent in multimedia offers. In 2015 the web will be overtaken by mobile devices. The 1.6 billion users on mobile devices will match the number of internet users accessing the internet through desktop computers. Users accessing the internet through mobile devices are expected to increase from 14 million in 2010 to 788 million in 2015. The revenue in mobile applications is anticipated to have increased from US$ 2.2 billion to US$ 37.5 billion. The amount of direct machine-to-machine communication is predicted to have increased 3.5-fold. The amount of data handled through the internet will continue to rapidly expand. A mere 20 homes connected to the internet in 2015 most likely will generate as much internet traffic as the whole World Wide Net in 1995.[2] IP traffic in 2015 probably will have quadrupled in comparison with 2010 and reach almost one zettabyte (10^{23}).[3]

In 2011 the United Nations declared access to broadband internet a basic human right, which elevated the web to the same level of importance as food and shelter.[4] Regional access to the internet will have changed too. Asia pacific will have taken the lead in internet traffic, followed by North America and Europe.[5]

But what do all these predictions have to do with communication of responsible business? Let's have a look at two unequal companies and their activities to communicate responsible business online. Consider for a moment the shoe and outdoor clothing maker, Timberland, versus the internet-giant Google. At first sight the two companies seem to be an unequal match. Shouldn't Google be able to surpass a smaller, lesser known business, in terms of online communication? You might be surprised.

Naturally you would use Google's very own search engine* to find out about what the company is doing in the social and environmental sphere, by searching for *Google sustainability*. A recent hit reflects an interview with Google's 26 year-old chief sustainability officer and former

Company:	Google
Industry:	Internet and software
Tool:	Online communication

Lesson: Communicating responsible business online successfully requires much more than technical infrastructure and know how.

---

* Search conducted February 18, 2012.

(Continued)

assistant of the company's co-founders, a key officer who hardly provides concise information on what the company is doing.[6] Other matches represent a mix of weakly related third-party blogs and completely unrelated information. Unsatisfied by the lack of hits, you might search for a more to-the-point *Google sustainability report*. Unfortunately, you will not find exactly what you have been looking for either. Five out of ten matches highlight the company's absence of a formalized sustainability performance report, using phrases such as being among the "top three laggards"[7] "F in sustainability reporting,"[8] and comment that "surprisingly" "*Google* is out of step with best practices."[9] The remaining "matches" are not related to the company's activities at all.

The negative impression of Google's commitment to sustainability is affirmed when looking closely at the corporate website. Where the vast majority of multinational businesses have a section dedicated to responsible business, Google seems to hide their information on the company's social and environmental business performance under, at best, weakly related headings. There are some fragments of information, such as information on healthy meals and employee well-being offers (headed "culture"), renewable energy usage (heading "about/ data centers," and philanthropic, social ventures, and the Google Green webpage, which highlights isolated, anecdotal blogs on Google and the environment (headed "initiatives").[10] Even after hours of search you will hardly find a webpage or document that display's Google's social and environmental performance in a well-structured and exhaustive way.

The lack of transparency and the unorganized sustainability information at Google seem unfortunate because Google has several advanced activities that are worth mentioning. More importantly, the world's leader in online communication has the technical potential and human know-how to do incredible good through the internet and to become an opinion leader for change toward a truly sustainable world. It might be time to change Google's unofficial mission "Don't be bad" to "do good."

If we evaluate a leading internet company's responsible business communication online as deficient, what can we expect of a bricks and mortar outdoor company, Timberland? Again you might be surprised.

Entering Timberland's corporate webpage you will not only find social and environmental topics integrated under each website heading, but also the "responsibility" section predominates in the website design. Entering into the section you will find a rich and well-organized world of information. Timberland organizes its sustainability information from

Company:	Timberland
Industry:	Outdoor clothing and footwear
Tool:	Online communication

Lesson: Good communication of responsible business online must be based on rich and qualitative content, excellent visibility, organization and integration of information, the possibility for stakeholders to personalize information and to engage with the company in a mutual, barrier-free and often playful exchange.

broad to specific in five main categories. First, the website lists a section on the company's broad commitment and journey toward sustainability, a description of the company's strategy and subsequent social and environmental performance indicators, and an extensive section covering reports with concise performance data. Information is also organized into the four main activity areas (climate, product, factories, and service), which and can be personalized through a "report builder" and allows stakeholders to interactively tailor the information received to the respective needs.[11]

For stakeholders who want to go a step further and constructively engage with the company, there is a gateway page to all of the company's "community" media featuring more than 15 ways to interact, such as Facebook, Twitter, and YouTube.[12] Timberland has managed to link and integrate its responsibility activities and communication with customers' private spheres, with its main business operations, and with its corporate image. Through attention-getting applications such as the "Hortiscope," Timberland educates customers about their environmental behavior and provides fun feedback. A highly entertaining quiz on Timberland's

(Continued)

Facebook page allows you to find out if you are a palm, oak, or maple tree.[13] Timberland also features a page for its "Earthkeepers" product line, which calls for heroes to save the planet with an extremely rich information mix of 3D animations, videos, wild music, an environmental life-cycle analysis of their shoes and an online shop.[14] The company blog features frequent calls for actions for interested stakeholders who can get active and collaborate with the company in responsible business topics.[15] For interested stakeholders, the highly interlinked online media make it easy to switch back and forth between the company's communication platforms for social and environmental business performance and receive the most from it.

As we have seen in practice, communicating with Stakeholders online can take a broad variety of different forms but also poses very specific challenges. In the following sections you will be introduced to the basics of successfully communicating online in responsible business.

Web Communication 1.0, 2.0, and 3.0

The World Wide Web is expanding to new regions of the world, to various socioeconomic classes, and for a multiplicity of uses. More importantly, the web is changing its very basic characteristics. The first (1.0) version of the web was a static, one-way information system. Users were rather passive recipients of information prepared by institutions with enough technical know-how and financial resources to establish a webpage. The possibilities to "communicate back" were restricted to email applications.

Web 2.0 brought a change from static to dynamic.[16] Users were empowered to be co-creators of many different kinds of content and applications such as video (e.g., YouTube), text (e.g., Blogger and Wordpress), and even software (e.g., the open source movement). The web also became mobile and omnipresent with an exponentially increasing number of mobile devices, which would often save information in the web "cloud" instead of on local devices. Web 2.0 also is characterized by its social component, where offline social life is massively transferred to online platforms such as Facebook and Twitter.

Web 3.0 currently is evolving from its 2.0 predecessor[17] to online activity that seems offline or "real-life." The distinction between the two spheres becomes increasingly blurred. A "metaverse," neither online, nor offline is created.[18] Through the online application "Foursquare," for instance, people can "log-in" to "physical" places such as the favorite pizzeria or an event online and let contacts know their actual location. The web becomes "intelligent" in a sense, that it detects users' behavior patterns and preferences and provides individually tailored contents, in a so-called "Filter Bubble." Google already tailors its search results to metadata of the individual.[19] At the same time the web becomes more standardized, through the "semantic web movement," aimed at creating a shared basic language, which can be accessed easily by both users and applications.

Don't get mixed up! Marketing 1.0, 2.0, 3.0

These three versions of marketing are highly related to the three distinct versions of the World Wide Web and to responsible business. Marketing 1.0 refers to activities based on the marketer as the main actor of the marketing management process. In marketing 2.0 marketers base their efforts on Web 2.0 tools such as social networks and mobile technologies. The definition of marketing 3.0 is counter-intuitive and does not refer to the usage of Web 3.0 for marketing. Instead, it refers to a new focus of marketing on wholeness and spirituality.[20]

As portrayed in Table 9.1, each version of the web brings advantages and challenges to communicating responsible business online, which can be observed when companies adapt a communication approach in the continuum between Web 1.0 and 3.0. The different types of web activity co-exist simultaneously, and companies can make active choices as to which type best suits the respective communication purpose in responsible business. A business, for example, that aims to co-create value with stakeholders will use a strong Web 2.0 strategy. This approach will maximize exchange and co-creation possibilities. A company in a crisis might want to achieve control over the contents shared on the web. This control would help mitigate reputational damage. The company would chose to communicate through a traditional web 1.0 homepage, which does not allow publicly visible reaction comments to be shared. A third company might aim to connect their real-life products to the virtual world through activities in the realm of Web 3.0. A good example is the joint Apple and Nike Pedometer application, which measures the number of steps taken by iPod users and allows them to connect to a personalized Nike training center online.[21] The case exemplifies how combined online-offline applications can be used to make a positive impact as part of a business's responsible business activity. The impact in this case is the increased health of people using the application.

Table 9.1. Main Advantages and Disadvantages of Communication Styles Related to the Various Web Versions

Type of web	Advantage	Disadvantage
1.0	Complete control over contents and answers	Restricted possibility for dialog and co-creation with stakeholders
2.0	Democratization of communication and enhanced possibility to interact with stakeholders	Unstructured and hard to grasp and control flow of information
3.0	Possibility to create real-life change and increase the eco-efficiency of lifestyles	Potential to block change for sustainable behaviors by keeping them in their own personalized world

How can a company communicate effectively in Web 2.0? The recommended set of communication practices described in Figure 9.1 has been derived from prominent features of Web 2.0 and from considerations assuming a responsible business communication perspective.

The four main elements of Figure 9.1 stem from the characteristics of Web 2.0. The two outer influence factors (real-life impact and self-personalization) are derived from Web 3.0 characteristics. It follows an illustration of the Web 2.0-related elements.

1. **Content quantity and quality**: In Web 2.0 "content is king." Both quality and quantity of content are crucially important. Differing from Web 1.0 where companies do need to create all contents themselves, Web 2.0 provides the opportunity for stakeholders to create related content. The main success factor for content creation lies in the co-creation of contents between companies and stakeholders, through Web 2.0 applications. The created contents must be

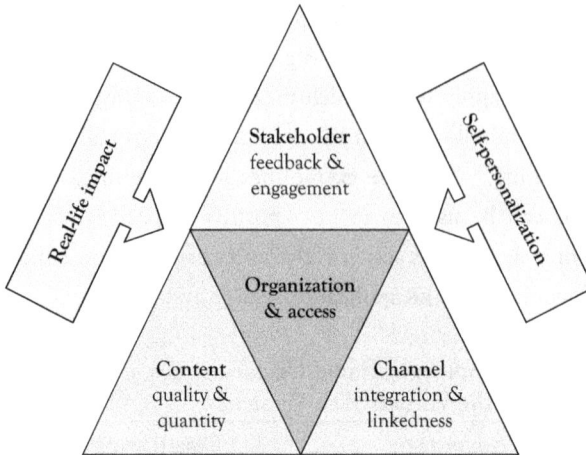

Figure 9.1. Characteristics of effective web communication in responsible business.

of high quality and credible to harness the viral characteristics of Web 2.0. A viral, "buzz" or mouth-to-mouth message is one that is sufficiently extraordinary to be passed on quickly and automatically once liberated by the communicator.[†]

2. **Channel integration and linking**: In Web 2.0, companies cannot rely on single communication channels, but must create an integrated and linked message throughout a diverse set of channels and jointly create the overall message of responsible business conduct. Importantly, the overall message must be consistent throughout all channels. It is also critical that the messages communicated by stakeholders and the business are mutually reinforcing. The Mexican branch Bancomer of the international bank BBVA produced its 2010 annual report on a memory stick to save paper and show responsible behavior. The "good news" was shared through Twitter. A significant number of stakeholders reacted to the news by tweeting about poor customer service, a latent issue which was more relevant to stakeholders than the USB delivered report. The two messages were highly contradictory.[22]

3. **Stakeholder feedback and engagement**: Web 2.0 applications, in particular social networks, can be used to get in touch and co-create

---

[†] Chapter 8 has provided more extensive coverage of buzz communication.

with stakeholders. The British newspaper, *The Guardian*, asked stake-holders to suggest topics for their sustainability report.[23] Jeans maker Levi asked stakeholders in a contest to design the best laundry rack after realizing that the biggest CO_2 life-cycle impact of their product is caused through the drying process in electric tumble dryers.[24] Levi's engaged stakeholders and co-created solutions to reduce one of the product's most severe negative environmental impacts.

4. **Organization and access**: All stakeholders of a company should be able to engage with the company online, and companies must actively reduce barriers to such engagement, including economic, technical, and knowledge barriers. Important stakeholders might not be able to engage online because they lack the financial resources to access the internet. They might not be able to use the technology or platform the company uses to communicate online. Facebook in China, for example, is used less than the local Baidu network. Or stakeholder might not know how to use applications or speak the language used by companies to communicate responsible business. Such exclusions are commonly known as "red-linings" which are sit-uations in which stakeholders are actively or passively denied access. In order to avoid denial of access to the communication process, companies must organize their online communication. The crucial question of how to avoid "net-lining" (red-lining over the internet) is "How can I organize my communication channels in order to give access to all groups that matter?" An excellent example of innovative organization and creation of access is cell phone-based banking in Kenya, where banks have teamed up with the British multinational communication company Vodafone to provide access to basic bank-ing services for remote communities.[25]

While the web moves from the 2.0 to 3.0 version, the preceding com-munication principles are valid but are complemented by the additional recommendations related to features of Web 3.0:

1. **Real-life impacts**: Web 3.0 exceeds the traditional boarders of the internet and has the potential to make impact in real life. P&G's *Future Friendly* webpage follows its goal to inspire consumers to use P&G's

product in a more environmental friendly way in their households. Web tools such as blogs with resource-saving tips, games and real-life competitions in the style of "Who can save the most water?" create positive environmental impacts in households all over the world.[26]

2. **Self-personalization**: A prominent feature of Web 3.0 applications is the capability to assess online behavior in order to self-personalize the contents provided to users. Google customizes search results based on previous searches and the internet user's metadata, such as location and information gathered in other Google applications. Two different Google users usually do not see the same results, even if conducting a completely identical search. Such self-personalization features are a mixed blessing. On one hand they may give users exactly what they want; on the other hand, the search might bar them from information. Communication in responsible business must facilitate change as one of its main tasks. If companies use self-personalization, companies could assure that contents provided to stakeholders are in line with the aspired change. Consumers entering a business' web page might be provided with information on new sustainable innovation prod-ucts, while investors would automatically see new socially responsible investment opportunities throughout the company's business units, and suppliers might automatically be informed about a new supplier sustainability program.

Online Communication Media for Responsible Business

Companies are making widespread use of Web 2.0 applications. A study among Fortune 100 companies reveals a constant growth trend. In 2011, 77 percent of those companies had Twitter accounts, 61 percent were on Facebook, 57 percent on YouTube, and at least 36 percent used corpo-rate blogs.[27] This snapshot of "fashionable" online media shows a growing trend to use online communication. In only one year, from 2010 to 2011 the use of those media had increased by 7 percent. The crucial question for businesses is: What is the online-media mix that communicates effec-tively to stakeholders? The following paragraphs provide an overview of typically used applications and technologies as well as an easy-to-apply process for online stakeholder communication management.

To effectively communicate responsible business online, we must first understand communicating online in general terms. Applications, technologies, and trends are constantly changing. Figure 9.2 shows how current applications can be categorized by their main functions. Tools focused on content primarily serve to create, organize, and share content, while interaction-focused tools facilitate the exchange between either individuals or machines. Tools focusing on applications resemble "machines" that fulfill a predefined task. The division chosen here is technical in a sense that categories are often overlapping and tools may share all three characteristics. Social networks, such as Facebook or LinkedIn, facilitate interaction between members, provide applications and games, and support the management of great amounts of contents, such as personal data and pictures. In the following paragraphs we provide a brief explanation of the main tools in each category and highlight how those tools can be used for communication in responsible business.

Content-Based Tools

The first group, **content-based tools** vary in form and shape from traditional corporate **websites.** Traditional websites certainly have their place

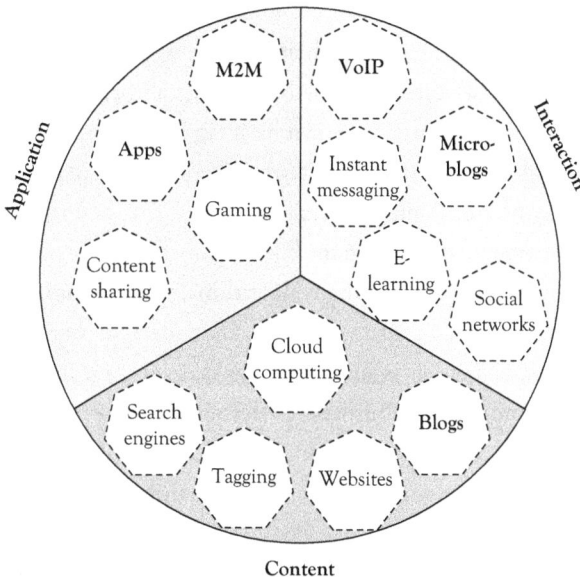

Figure 9.2. Classification of web tools.

in the online stakeholder communication portfolio. These websites are often used as gateway sites to provide a structured overview and entry point to the company's other online media. Corporate websites are also the typical location for sustainability reports and tools that communicate in a one-way fashion. A content-based tool called **tagging** fulfills the function of bookmarking, marking or tagging contents with keywords, in order to make them found. Tags are *metadata* that allows users to understand the structure and content of a document without the need to review it. Defining the right tags for contents is a crucial task. Contents such as videos, pictures, or whole written documents might remain invisible for users, no-matter how relevant the content might be. The most impressive video on YouTube, for instance, describing your company's advanced responsible business activities will not find a great audience if it is not tagged with the right terms (e.g., sustainability, philanthropy, corporate responsibility, and of course your company name).

Through the process of social tagging, users who are not creators of content can add tags and create a *folksonomy*, which can then serve to identify or specify contents even if the content creator did not do so. Social tagging also serves to correct tags that do not reflect the true structure of the content or which might have been chosen misleading on purpose by the content creator. A special use of tags are so-called *hash tags,* used mostly in microblogging sites such as Twitter, where the tag is included with a hash sign (#) directly into the text to categorize it. To increase interactivity, you can create your own hash tag describing your company's main responsibility program. This tag can be used by other users to talk about what you are doing. General Electric (GE), for instance, did so with their Ecomagination program.[28]

As an important part of their algorithms, **search engines**, such as Google and Yahoo look up tags. For a company that wants to be recognized as responsible, it is important for users to find information on social and environmental business performance when searching either for the company in general or even more importantly when searching for information on responsible business. The aforementioned search for Google's sustainability report is a good example of search engine usage went wrong. Instead of listing positive hits, the search report revealed negative content.

To ensure users see search results the company wants to communicate, it can apply *search engine optimization (SEO)*, which manages content actively to appear on top of the list of Google or other search engines. Strategies that companies typically apply are the creation of massive amounts of content and user traffic, the use of concise tags, and the creation of links to other sites. Those factors are important elements in the search engines' algorithm to identify relevant results. To reduce the visibility of negative online publicity in crisis communication, companies should avoid directly answering or linking to critical sites because this action increases their search engine visibility. Instead companies should take the strategy to create positive contents that displace the "bad news" and to comment back on their own sites, without directly linking to the critical sources. SEO creates content-based strategies for visibility, while *search engine marketing (SEM)* provides a paid positioning of your company or product among search results.

Socialmention.com is a very attractive search engine to see whether stakeholders are receiving the same message of a responsible business that your company is sending. The website not only searches where your company is mentioned throughout social webpages, such as Facebook and Twitter, but also analyses what others say about you in the categories strength (coverage in social media), sentiment (positive or negative), passion (emphasis and feelings), and reach (number of distinct authors).[29] Comparing the two outdoor companies Timberland and Patagonia, which are both known for their strong responsible business activities, the four categories are almost identical, although Timberland seems to evoke stronger feelings about its company. While Patagonia scores 24 percent in passion, Timberland scores 62 percent. On the other hand, Patagonia scores 12:1 in the relationship between positive and negative comments on the company, while Timberland has only a slightly positive score of 3:1.[‡] Interestingly, a comparative search for BP, despite the company's history of the Gulf of Mexico oil spill, shows the same 3:1 relationship between positive and negative comments as observed for Timberland.

[‡] Searches were conducted 21.02.2012 with the search terms Timberland Company, Patagonia Company, and British Petroleum Company.

Another excellent method is **blogs**, which are periodically updated text-based blogs (or video-based Vlogs and audio-based podcasts). Twitter blogs often appear as entries at the top of searches because they are text-rich and attract constant traffic from recurrent users or followers. The company Genomma Labs had been largely criticized for promoting in 2011 so-called miracle products with questionable health effects. Nevertheless, a Google search[§] with the company name revealed only one out of 11 posts that referred to the issue of miracle drugs. This match was the last one on the search page. The posts that displaced the negative publicity are mainly related to the company's blogs, of which many are related to socially responsible activities of the company.

Microblogs, which consist of short text-based messages around 140 characters, are a distinct form of blogs. The best-known microblog is Twitter, which has found extensive commercial application. The company Best Buy primarily manages the relationship with its customer stakeholders through Twitter.[30] Timberland uses Twitter to communicate with a broader set of stakeholders.[31] Microblogs, due to the limitation to short texts and the importance of the close relationship with followers, are less content-driven and more interaction- focused than traditional blogs.

Cloud-computing refers to transferring applications, platforms, and infrastructure from local computers to the internet, referring to the hard to grasp cloud of online computing. Cloud computing is an important enabler of mobile computing because devices can save size, energy and other technical requirements when they become pure gateways to computing services provided in the net. Cloud computing has been described as more environmental friendly than traditional computing because of increased energy efficiency; an assumption which still requires additional proof.[32]

Application-Based Tools

The second group, **application-based tools,** is labeled counter-intuitively. Any online tool is based on some kind of application, but the ones introduced in the following section refer to applications that fulfill very specific

---

[§] Search date: 15.01.2012

and clearly delimited tasks for users. Most obviously falling into this category are so-called **Apps** (short for online application software), which can be used by companies to either communicate their own responsible business activity or to enhance their responsible management practices. An App that fits into both categories is provided by sourcemap.com, which companies can use to visualize the environmental impact of transportation of their products. For instance the shoe company TOMS described in preceding chapters impressively shows impacts of both their upstream and downstream transportation activities of shoes to consumers and donated shoes to "shoe-drops" in third-world countries.[33] The "baa code" by sheep-wool clothing producer Icebreaker includes an app on their webpage that allows consumers to use a bar-code provided with the purchase of their product to trace back the source of the product to single-sheep ranches.[34] There are also many apps for mobile devices designed to make a sustainable life easier for individuals. Prominent examples include tools to identify the nearest recycling facility, sustainably sourcing seafood restaurants, and eco-touristic resorts.[35]

Content sharing tools share various types of content including video (e.g., Youtube, Vimeo), audio (e.g., I-Tunes, Audiofarm), and presentations (e.g., Prezi, Slideshare). Content sharing may be available to the general public or privately. Content sharing should not be confused with **machine-to-machine communication (M2M)**, which is an important feature of Web 3.0. The potential to facilitate more eco-efficient living patterns in M2M communication is immense. Imagine a future, where your mobile phone via GPS detects that you have left your residence and tells your residence's electronic devices such as air conditioning and lights to turn off. Imagine your refrigerator reading RFC tags on the food you bought, warning you about soon expiring items, and asking your computer to search online for cooking recipes based on the food still available, which will then be sent to your mobile phone. In both examples, unnecessary environmental impact (e.g., CO_2 emissions, water usage, packaging) have been avoided through the intelligent M2M communication mechanisms. For a responsible company, such a pattern does not involve active human communication effort, but requires making products compatible with such systems.

Gaming applications are more complex than the web apps described before in responsible business, providing a playful way to engage stakeholders in social and environmental topics. Games are characterized by win or lose situations or rankings between players. Games, depending upon the degree of interaction, may be categorized as single- or multiplayer games. Timberland uses a game on Facebook named Virtual Forest. Players compete against other players in building a forest; and for each tree planted in this virtual forest, Timberland plants a real tree in Haiti, which is suffering from a long history of deforestation.[36] The process of *gamification* refers to engaging audiences in a fun way to solve problems. The central idea is to engage people to solve sustainability problems that unleash their creative potential.[37] An example for such a world-changing game is the multiplayer mass-collaboration simulation game *World without Oil*, which requires players to develop coping strategies during the first 30 days of an oil crisis. As a consequence players learn how to reduce their dependence on oil in real life.[38]

Interaction Tools

The third group, **interaction-based tools** are the basis of the core feature *co-creation* in Web 2.0. Simple two-way interaction is provided by **Instant Messaging (IM)** and **Voice over Internet Protocol (VoIP)** applications, which both provide effective web-based communication models. Both applications may be used to increase the quality of distance-communication and might be served to substitute CO_2-intensive business trips by web-meetings. The main public VoIP service Skype offers for free, high-quality conferencing functions. Communication service providers, such as AVAYA support *teleworking* through web-based technologies and aim to reduce the environmental impact of commuting.[39]

E-learning tools and virtual workplaces are an excellent means to achieve the same positive effects of reducing environmental impacts of travelling mentioned before. E-learning and virtual workplace tools can be broadly divided into content-*management platforms*, which often also include rudimentary communication functions, such as blogs and e-mail. Those platforms also allow to manage participants by providing them with different roles, rights and responsibilities and enabling them to join groups. Content management platforms are geared toward asynchronous communication. Prominent examples for such content-management platforms are the free tool Moodle and the paid service Blackboard.

Virtual class and meeting rooms instead focus on synchronous communication through voice, webcam, presentation, chat, and a variety of additional services, which enable class organization or a meeting in virtual space. Tools typically used include Adobe Connect, WebEx, and Elluminate. E-learning may be an option for your organization both as provider and as recipient of contents related to responsible business. The organization Net Impact has an open database of recorded and scheduled life webinars, most of them for free, which are an excellent source for hands-on experience and skills to manage responsible business.[40]

Probably the most discussed collaboration-based web tools are **social network sites (SNS)**. The core features of SNS are the creation of an at least partly public personal **profile,** sharing of **connections** with other users, and **viewing of** one's own and other's connections.[41]

Recently such networks have become much more content-focused through the integration of other web tools with SNS. Users can access pictures, videos, documents and other contents. These networks also increasingly embed applications and games, such as Timberland's tree-planting application mentioned before. The concrete configuration of a specific network depends on the intended usage. Distinctions to be made are between vocational-professional networks (e.g., LinkedIn, Xing) and private ones (e.g., Facebook, Xaidu), between topic-centered *vertical* and personal-relationship-centered *horizontal networks.* A vertical SNS such as Facebook builds itself around the personal relationship of users, while vertical networks are built around specific topics and users' expertise in those topics. Ning provides the possibility to tailor make an "own" social network for a specific topic. For instance the Ning network *Development Crossing* is a global network that focuses exclusively on responsible and sustainable business topics, which has been established through the Ning platform.[42] Companies can use such a personalized SNS to engage more closely with stakeholders.

The following recommendations are offered for helping companies successfully communicate responsible business using social networks:

- **Create content and add value**: Adding value and content in social networks is key. To build relationship with stakeholders, companies have to offer added value, such as applications, interesting information, visual elements, inspiration, or the feeling of belonging. The more value you add on a social network, the more likely is that the value will be shared and evokes a so-called buzz, where your content is shared rapidly among users.

- **Interact, receive, and always respond**: Social networks live from the interaction. Once you have created contents and related relationship, start moving! Ask contacts about their opinion, ask to create related contents, and provoke reaction. If users get in touch with you, always respond. There is nothing worse than someone with a "disappointed love" who starts campaigning against you.

- **Plan, but give up control**: Social networks, answers, and opinions cannot be controlled. If your goal is to create a predefined image, do not use social networks. A social network strategy requires envisioning many scenarios based on potential reactions to what you do. It is crucial to deal successfully with critical comments. Communication channels in social networks are always open and they operate quickly.

- **Engage strategically**: In SNS, 90 percent of users are lurkers, who read, observe, and do not contribute. Nine percent are users that contribute from time to time, and only one percent are heavy contributors.[43] A social network strategy must define this active one percent of users and engage with them in order to reach the passive 90 percent.

This section aimed at providing an overview of technologies and platforms typically used online. In the next section, you will see how to connect those to a consistent responsible business online communication strategy, to manage the online communication process, and to deploy specialized responsible business web communication activities.

The Online Communication Process

The process of communicating online is not very different from communication through traditional media and progresses through a similar sequence of stages as described in Figure 9.3.[44] What is different about online communication are the activities required to successfully complete each stage.

For instance, the communicator must specify in the **goal** setting stage which of the three communication purposes mentioned in Chapter 1 (definition, implementation, or sharing of the message about responsible business) is pursued by the communication activities. This first step is of crucial importance, as it serves to define the subsequent communication strategy and is the basis for developing an effective measurement and control method for communication outcomes. The following guidelines can aid companies in assessing their communication purposes and setting goals.

- **Define your responsible business activity by observing stakeholder participation**. Your assessment of goals and indicators to measure the fulfillment of the communication purpose must be much more than a mere number of clicks or views. One metric can be the number of community members actively posting ideas if you take a social network as communication media. A good example for such an exchange is the Germany-based *Utopia* platform, which is a mixed

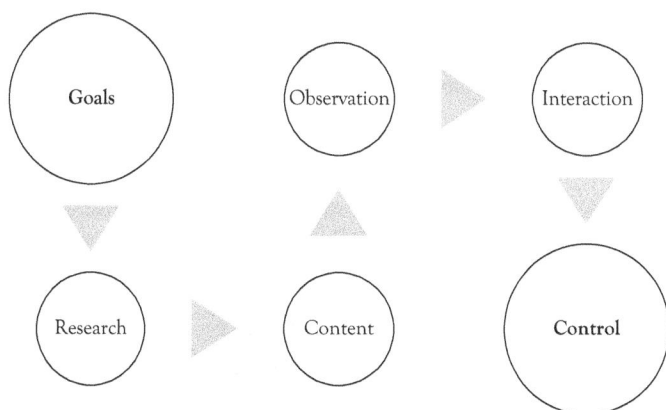

Figure 9.3. The online communication process.

company-consumer platform for strategic consumption. Both parties in *Utopia* can become involved into a mutual exchange and utilize various analysis tools in the interaction.

- **Make sure your goals reflect the use of online communication to support the implementation process of responsible business**. Consumer packaged goods companies such as P&G might start an online survey among the users of their *Future Friendly* webpage to see what percentage of customers actually changed their behavior to more environmental friendly usage of the company's products. Such a survey might also ask for the environmental impact reductions, such as savings in water, energy (CO_2), and waste.

- **Use website analytics programs such as Google Analytics to spread the word about your responsible business activity.** These programs allow you to track the number of clicks per content published or the views of a video on YouTube and to count the number of subscribers to blogs or followers on Twitter. Samsung Electronics measured the cumulative visitors to the company's responsible business blog, titled *Samsung Tomorrow*. The total visitors surpassed 800,000 and Twitter followers reached 40,000, as of December 2010.[45]

To maximize effectiveness of online communication measures, it is necessary to apply **research** to understand both the intended recipients of your communication and their online behavior and preferences. Research results serve primarily to define the online communication medium used and the types of contents created to fulfill stakeholder need and the businesses' communication goals. If you want to convince key decision makers, such as international experts in sustainability knowledgeable of your company, you might want to consider that only 26 percent of those individuals trust in social networks for such information, and 53 percent say that social networks do not influence their decisions at all. Most (75 percent) international sustainability experts indicate that they trust in independently verified labels.[46] In this case online communication makes sense as a communication tool for spreading the word about external endorsement of responsible business labels.

Deciding what **contents** are created in online communication depends on the stakeholders targeted by communication activities and on the online communication platform used. Contents and platforms used can vary widely from text contents in blogs, to applications, to audio contents as podcasts. BP, following the oil spill caused by the company's drilling platform Deepwater Horizon, created a special YouTube channel entitled *Gulf Stories*, which dealt with on-topic news.[47] From a crisis communication point of view, it seemed good to choose a video-based communication platform. Taken together with an online sustainability report on the corporate webpage both platforms allowed for only limited feedback.

Once you have done your research homework and created contents, it is time to get online. Nevertheless, the initial activity should be the one of an observer, not yet a communicator. **Observing** other company's communication activities and stakeholders' reactions online might be time consuming, but it is worth the effort in order to get it right from the beginning. Early communication mistakes are often hard to fix and cannot be taken back once the word is out in the virtual space. The purpose in this stage is to learn from success and to avoid typical online communication trapdoors.

Companies may learn much from an episode related to McDonald's attempt to Twitter "good news stories" through a #McDStories hashtag. As the story goes, the hashtag was soon flooded by McDonald's critical stakeholders communicating bad news and stories about the company.[48] Of course this did not fulfill the company's communication purpose of spreading the good news. The learning effect from "eavesdropping" on companies that are similar to the eavesdropper's company is probably bigger than from observing completely unrelated companies.

Once you know the terrain, it is time to start **communicating** online. For effective online communication you can apply the same criteria applied in Chapter 2, as well as the six points mentioned in the first part of this chapter. The online communication cycle closes with **controlling** the goals set at the beginning and readjusting the communication strategy based on those results.

To support and catalyze the online communication process for responsible business, it is important to note the following online communication activities that are of special importance to responsible business:

- **Online sustainability reporting**: The time of printed reports is over. Printing is resource intensive in many respects and impractical to handle for stakeholders. Advanced online reporting technologies allow for quick availability and easy handling. They also may be increasingly personalized, allowing stakeholders to select specific information and to use a wide additional variety of online resources. Such resources include videos, instant feedback channels, and extensive databases that cannot be provided through a print report. An upcoming feature in online reporting is real-time coverage, in which companies leave the once-a-year reporting pattern and instead provide fresh and frequently updated information throughout the traditional categories covered in a sustainability report[*].

- **Crowdsourcing and crowdfunding**: Harnessing the immense and well-connected "online crowd" to provide solutions is called *crowdsourcing*.[49] Crowdsourcing has primarily been used for R&D and design tasks, but increasingly provides attractive solutions in responsible business such as Levi's design challenge, and The Guardian's sustainability report design campaign.[50] One of the biggest crowdsourcing campaigns in responsible business is the Pepsi *Refresh Project*, an online campaign that invited users to find solutions to social and environmental problems. The campaign distributed grants between 5000 and 250,000 USD for the best solutions between 2010 and 2011 and had received 7.5 million likes on Facebook[**].[51] *Crowdfunding* works similar to crowdsourcing, but asks the online crowd for funding instead of ideas.[52] The purpose of the mechanism is to receive small amounts of

---

[*] See Chapter 6 for extensive information on sustainability reporting.
[**] Figure based on research conducted 23.02.2012.

money from many individuals through the use of social networks or similar online media.[53] Crowdfunding is a promising strategy especially for social and environmental entrepreneurs because of the emotional capital of such businesses. People of the crowd may fund a venture either through donations, loans, or by becoming co-owners similar to traditional cooperative business models.[54]

- For instance, the baby products company Munchkin started the campaign "send a duck, raise a buck" which is a form of indirect crowd funding (the company pays, based on actions of the crowd), in which the company donates to a cancer foundation every time someone sends a virtual company branded rubber duck to friends online.[55]

- **Online activism and real-life linkages**: In 2010, the scandal around the Wikileaks platform, which made information from the business and governmental world public, shed light on the internet's potential as a platform for large scale activism and its tangible real life outcomes.[56] Examples of online activism attacking companies' specific irresponsible activities are many. Nike in 2001 entered into an interesting exchange with activist Eric Zorn, who asked the company to stitch the word "Sweatshop" on his sneakers. Nike at this time offered the online customization service Nike iD, which offered personalized shoes with a customized text.[57] The German website Regenwald.org (translated Rainforest.org) informs about corporate and governmental behavior around the world that threatens rainforests and asks individuals to sign a petition online. This petition is then forwarded to respective businesses and governments around the world.[58] The online activity has already resulted in several legislative outcomes with true real-life impacts. Companies communicating online must consider online activism. The goal is supporting real-life impacts for a more sustainable world rather than becoming activists' target.

Summary

Online communication for responsible business can be very effective and should thus become a center part of a responsible business communication strategy. In this chapter you have considered a set of six principles for effective online communication in an online world characterized by Web 1.0, 2.0, and 3.0 features. You have also been presented with an overview of online communication tools fulfilling content, interaction, and application-related functions. Finally, you have learned how to manage the online communication process and how to use online communication activities that are specifically meaningful to responsible business such as online reporting, activism, and crowd sourcing.

Put it to Practice!

Assess your own organization on each of the following elements of the stakeholder communication process:

Task	Assessment
(A) **Define communication goals**: My company has clearly defined the communication goals of current online communication activities and defined indicators to track the fulfillment of those goals.	
(B) **Research**: My company understands the online behavior of the stakeholders targeted through online communication.	
(C) **Content**: My company has developed unique and attractive contents that add value for the targeted stakeholder group.	
(D) **Observation**: My company has observed the online behavior of similar businesses and the reactions of stakeholders to such behavior.	
(E) **Interaction**: My company is consistently and proactively interacting with the targeted stakeholder online.	
(F) **Control**: My company controls the achievement of predefined communication goals and adjusts the online communication strategy based on the results achieved.	

Notes

Chapter 1

1. United Nations Environment Programme (2006).
2. Freeman (1984), p. 25.
3. TOMS (2011); TOMS Shoes (2009); TOMS (2012).
4. Waller & Conaway (2011).
5. Palmquist (2010).
6. TCCC (2011).
7. Carroll (1999).
8. Elkington (1998).
9. Brundtland (1987).
10. Laasch & Flores (2010).
11. Yunus (2010).
12. Austin & Reficco (2009).
13. SustainAbility (2008).
14. Samsung (2012).
15. Ibid, p. 5.
16. Ibid, p. 8.
17. Ibid, p. 15.
18. Ibid, p. 60.
19. Laasch & Conaway (2012).
20. Laasch & Conaway (2012).
21. TOMS Shoes (2009).
22. AccountAbility (2011), p. 8.

Chapter 2

1. Horiuchi, Schuchard, Shea, & Townsend (2009).
2. Starbucks (2011).
3. Starbucks (2009).
4. Lozanova (2009).
5. Starbucks Global Responsibility Report (2010).
6. FSBA (2012).
7. Hoovers, (2011).

8. Emsden (2012).
9. LensCrafters (2011).
10. OneSight (2011).
11. AMA (2007).
12. (2006).
13. Sherman et al. (2006).
14. Sherman et al. (2006), p. 13.
15. Iezzi, (2008), p.16.
16. (1948).
17. (2012).
18. (2011).
19. (2011).
20. Yahoo! Finance (2011).
21. Jargon (2011).
22. (2011).

Chapter 3

1. Du, Bhattacharya, & Sen (2007), p. 229.
2. Prahalad (2010).
3. CEMEX (2011).
4. CEMEX; ITESM; World Bank (2011).
5. Thoma (2011).
6. Der Spiegel (2008).
7. Accountability (2011).
8. Savage, Nix, Whitehead, & Blair (1991); Mitchel, Agle, & Wood (1997).
9. The Local (2009).
10. Morsing & Schultz (2006).
11. AMA (2007).
12. Thorson & Moore (1996), p. 18.
13. Samsung (2012).
14. Kotler & Lee (2004).
15. CEMEX (2011).
16. Laasch & Conaway (2011).
17. Brubaker (2005).
18. Story (2008).
19. Cahal Milmo (2006).
20. Porter (1985).
21. Prahalad (2010).
22. Walmart (2010).

Chapter 4

1. Ethics Resource Center (2011), p. 4.
2. Institute for Crisis Management (2011).
3. Greenburg & Elliott (2009), p. 190.
4. Taubken & Leibold (2010).
5. (2008).
6. (2010).
7. ERC (2011).
8. Ethics Resource Center (2011).
9. Jargon (2011).
10. Jargon, 2011.
11. (2009).
12. Coombs (2011).
13. Coombs (2002).
14. Bussey (2011).
15. (2012).
16. Torry & Sherr (2012).
17. (1980).
18. Ibid, p. 133.
19. Bloomberg's Businessweek (2009).
20. p. 213.
21. (2011).
22. (2011).
23. (2011).
24. (2011).
25. Ethics Resource Center (2011).

Chapter 5

1. Hitt, Ireland, & Hoskisson (2011).
2. DJSI (2011).
3. Automobile Magazine (2012).
4. BMW Objectives, Key Facts, and Figures (2010).
5. BMW Annual Report (2011).
6. Procter and Gamble (2011).
7. Coca Cola 2020 Vision (2012).
8. PepsiCo Vision (2012).
9. Coca Cola Sustainability (2012).
10. Lewis (2000).

11.   (2011).
12.   Makower (2010).
13.   Procter and Gamble (2011).
14.   Toyota Global Vision (2012).
15.   (2010).
16.   Ibid, p. 228.
17.   Toyota US Vision (2012).
18.   Walmart (2011).
19.   Walmart (2012).
20.   Walmart (2012).
21.   Freeman (2010).
22.   Williams (2008).
23.   Procter and Gamble Mission Statement (2012).
24.   Toyota USA (2012).
25.   Cengage (2012).
26.   (2008).
27.   (1987).
28.   (1989).
29.   Westpac Bank (2012).
30.   Westpac Bank (2012).
31.   DJSI Westpac (2012).
32.   DJSI Brazil (2011).
33.   DJSI Lotte (2011).
34.   Lotte Sustainability Report (2011).
35.   UN Global Compact (2011).
36.   Walmart Sustainability (2012).
37.   (2010).
38.   Sobczak (2006).
39.   Nijhof, Cludts, Fisscher, & Laan (2003).
40.   Ethical Trading Initiative (2012).
41.   Nike Code of Conduct (2012).
42.   Nike Code of Conduct (2012).

Chapter 6

1.   Thurm, R. (2010), p. 109.
2.   Obama (2012).
3.   DJSI Information (2012).
4.   CNN Money (2011).
5.   Itaúsa Information (2012).
6.   DJSI Brazil (2011).

7. (2012).
8. Itaúsa Annual Sustainability Report (2010).
9. (2009).
10. SIGMA Project Guidelines (2012).
11. Michael Baldinger, CEO, SAM (2012).
12. Fairtrade Monitoring (2011), p. 6.
13. Sekem (2012).
14. Seelos & Mair (2004).
15. Seelos & Mair (2004), p. 7.
16. Seelos & Mair (2004), p. 18.
17. Clorox Reporting (2012).
18. Larsen & Toubro (2012).
19. GRI Information (2012).
20. GRI Sustainability Reporting Guidelines, p. 2.
21. Margolis & Gomes Casseres (2012).

Chapter 7

1. Greenbiz.com (2012).
2. (2009).
3. Innocent (2012).
4. Innocent Kids (2012).
5. Innocent (2012).
6. (2011).
7. Belz and Peattie (2009), p. 203.
8. Glaxosmithkline (2012).
9. United Airlines (2012).
10. Lovell (2007).
11. Lovell (2007).
12. UPS (2012).
13. (2012).
14. PUMA (2012).
15. Varadarajan & Menon (1988).
16. TOMS (2012).
17. RED (2012).
18. Susan B. Komen (2012).
19. Newman's Own (2012).
20. Armstrong & Kotler (2009).
21. The Fun Theory (2012).
22. Procter and Gamble (2008).
23. Belch and Belch (2009), p. 147.

24. Stages adapted from Belch and Belch (2009), chapter 5.
25. Weinreich (2011).
26. LOHAS (2012).

Chapter 8

1. Knapp & Hall (2010).
2. Taylor (2006).
3. Celebrity Cars (2011).
4. Andidas (2003).
5. Halbright & Dunn (2010).
6. Innocent (2012).
7. Armitstead (2009).
8. Baker (2007); Greenpeace (2010).
9. TOMS Shoes (2009).
10. Carl (2006).
11. CNN Money (2011).
12. Greenwald (2005).
13. LEGO (2012a); LEGO Group (2010).
14. LEGO (2012b).
15. Chamberlain (2011).
16. LEGO (2011).
17. CNN Money (2011).
18. Clark (2002).
19. Hasbro (2012).
20. Fields (2009).
21. Lutts (1992).
22. LEGO (2012c).
23. Cinépolis (2008).
24. TOMS Shoes (2012).
25. PepsiCo (2012).
26. The Food & Drink Innovation Network (2011).
27. Earthimprints (2011).
28. Danone (2010).

Chapter 9

1. Lundquist (2010), p. 1.
2. Leopoldo (2011).
3. Webster (2011).

4. Lane (2011).
5. Barnett (2011).
6. Keefe (2008).
7. Raftery (2010).
8. Environmental Leader (2008).
9. Kron (2008).
10. Google (2012).
11. Timberland (2011).
12. Timberland (2012a).
13. Timberland (2012b).
14. Timberland (2012c).
15. Timberland (2012d).
16. O'Reilly (2005).
17. Agarwal (2009); Hendler (2009); Lassila & Hendler (2007).
18. Smart (2007).
19. Pariser (2011).
20. Kotler, Kartajaya, & Setiawan (2010).
21. Apple (2012).
22. Lopez & Martinez (2012).
23. Confino (2010).
24. Levi Strauss (2010).
25. Jack & Suri (2010).
26. Procter & Gamble (2011a); Procter & Gamble (2011b).
27. Burson-Marsteller (2011).
28. General Electric (2012).
29. Social Mention (2012).
30. Best Buy (2012).
31. Timberland (2012e).
32. Fuchs (2008).
33. Sourcemap (2012).
34. Icebreaker (2012).
35. Clark (2011).
36. Timberland (2012f).
37. Peters (2011).
38. Eklund (2012).
39. Avaya (2009).
40. Net Impact (2011).
41. Boyd & Ellison (2008).
42. Development Crossing (2012).
43. Nielsen (2006).
44. Lopez & Martinez (2012).

45. Samsung (2012).
46. SustainAbility (2011).
47. BP (2012).
48. Guardian (2012a).
49. Howe, 2006; Brabham (2008).
50. Massey (2011).
51. PepsiCo (2012).
52. Belleflamme, Lambert, & Schwienbacher (2011).
53. Sullivan (2006).
54. Given (2011); Schwienbacher & Larralde (2010).
55. Keene (2007).
56. Guardian (2012b).
57. Zweifel (2001).
58. Regenwald (2012).

References

AccountAbility. (2011a). *AA1000 Stakeholder engagement standard 2011: Final exposure draft.* London: AccountAbility.

Accountability. (2011b). *AccountAbility: Setting the standard for corporate responsibility and sustainable development.* Retrieved November 20, 2011, from http://www.accountability.org/

Agarwal, A. (2009). *Web 3.0 concepts explained in plain English (presentations).* Retrieved February 23, 2012, from Digital Inspiration: http://www.labnol.org/internet/web-3-concepts-explained/8908/

American Marketing Association. (2007). *Definition of marketing.* Retrieved February 12, 2012, from American Marketing Association: http://www.marketingpower.com/AboutAMA/Pages/DefinitionofMarketing.aspx

Andidas. (2003). *Toyota prius; marketing communications plan.* London: Andidas.

Ansoff, I. (1980). Strategic issue management. *Strategic Management Journal, 1*(2), 131–148.

Armitstead, L. (2009). *Is innocent still the real thing?* Retrieved March 2, 2012, from The Telegraph: http://www.telegraph.co.uk/finance/newsbysector/retailandconsumer/5140410/Is-Innocent-still-the-real-thing.html

Armstrong, G., & Kotler, P. (2009). *Marketing: An introduction.* Upper Saddle River, NJ: Pearson Education, Inc.

Atkins, S. (1999). *Cause related marketing: Who cares wins.* Oxford: Butterworth-Heinemann.

Austin, J., & Reficco, E. (2009). Corporate social entrepreneurship. *HBS Working Paper Series, 101*(9), 1–8.

Automobile Magazine. (2012). *First look: 2013 BMW megacity vehicle.* Retrieved June 21, 2012, from http://www.automobilemag.com/green/news/1007_2013_bmw_megacity_vehicle/index.html

Avaya. (2009). *Product operation and end of life management.* Retrieved February 28, 2012, from Avaya: http://www.avaya.com/gcm/master-usa/en-us/topics/sustainability/information/productoperations.htm

Baker, M. (2007). *British Petroleum.* Retrieved October 15, 2011, from Mallenbaker.net: http://www.mallenbaker.net/csr/CSRfiles/bp.html

Barnett, T. (2011). *Global internet expansion: Who will lead the way?* Retrieved February 16, 2012, from CISCO: http://blogs.cisco.com/news/global-internet-expansion-who-will-lead-the-way/

Barton, L. (1993). *Crisis in organizations: Managing and communicating in the heat of crisis.* Nashville: Southwestern Publishers.

Belch, G. E., & Belch, M. A. (2009). *Advertising and promotion: An integrated marketing communications perspective* (8th ed.). Boston, MA: McGraw-Hill/Irwin.

Belleflamme, P., Lambert, T., & Schwienbacher, A. (2011). Crowdfunding: Tapping the right crowd. *Center for Operations Research Discussion Paper Series*, p. 32.

Belz, F. M., & Peattie, K. (2009). *Sustainability marketing: A global perspective.* Glasgow, England: John Wiley & Sons, Ltd.

Best Buy. (2012). *@BestBuy*. Retrieved February 24, 2012, from Twitter: http://twitter.com/#!/bestbuy

Bloomberg. (2012). Retrieved February 15, 2012, from http://www.bloomberg.com/quote/ITSA4:BZ

Bloomberg Businessweek. (2009). Retrieved February 15, 2012, from http://www.businessweek.com/the_thread/brandnewday/archives/2009/04/dominos_pizza_y.html

Bloomberg Businessweek. (2012). Retrieved February 15, 2012, from http://www.businessweek.com/smallbiz/content/jan2009/sb20090123_264702.htm

BMW (2010). *Objectives, key facts, and figures.* Retrieved February 2, 2012, from http://www.bmwgroup.com/bmwgroup_prod/e/0_0_www_bmwgroup_com/verantwortung/svr_2010/_pdf/11670_SVR_2010_engl_Objectives_Key_Facts_and_Figures.pdf

BMW Annual Report. (2011). Retrieved February 2, 2012, from http://annual-report2011.bmwgroup.com/bmwgroup/annual/2011/gb/English/pdf/report2011.pdf

Boyd, D. M., & Ellison, N. B. (2008). Social network sites: Definition, history, and scholarship. *Computer-Mediated Communication, 13*(1), 210–230.

British Petroleum. (2012). *Official BP channel.* Retrieved February 28, 2012, from Youtube: http://www.youtube.com/user/BPplc?ob=0&feature=results_main

Brabham, D. C. (2008). Crowdsourcing as a model for problem solving. *Convergence 14*(1), 75–90.

British Broadcasting Corporation. (2011). *Who, what, why: How could Reebok sell trainers for $1?* Retrieved November 26, 2011, from http://www.bbc.co.uk/news/magazine-15873765

Brubaker, H. (2005). *Wal-Mart switches to corn-based plastic packaging.* Retrieved February 2, 2012, from Environmental News Network: http://www.enn.com/top_stories/article/13175

Brundtland, G. H. (1987). *Presentation of the report of the World Comission on Environment and Development to UNEP's 14th governing council.* Nairobi, Kenya. June 8, 1987.

Burson-Marsteller. (2011). *2011 Fortune global 100 social media study.* Retrieved February 24, 2012, from Burson-Marsteller: http://www.burson-marsteller.com/Innovation_and_insights/blogs_and_podcasts/BM_Blog/Lists/Posts/Post.aspx?ID=254

Bussey, J. (2011). Measuring the human cost of an iPad made in China, *The Wall Street Journal*. Retrieved June 21, 2012, from www.wsj.com

Cahal Milmo. (2006). *Body Shop's popularity plunges after L'Oreal sale.* Retrieved February 12, 2012, from The Independent: http://www.independent. co.uk/news/uk/this-britain/body-shops-popularity-plunges-after-loreal-sale-473599.html

Carl, W. J. (2006). What's all the buzz about? Everyday communication and the relational basis of word-of-mouth and buzz marketing practices. *Management Communication Quarterly 19*(4), 601–634.

Carroll, A. B. (1999). Corporate social responsibility a definitional construct. *Business & Society 38*(3), 268–295.

Carroll, A. B., & Buchholtz, A. K. (2009). *Business and society: Ethics and stakeholder management* (7th ed.). Mason, OH: Cengage Publishers.

Celebrity Cars. (2011). *How many stars own a prius?* Retrieved March 1, 2012, from Celebrity Cras Blog: http://www.celebritycarsblog.com/2011/01/how-many-celebrities-drive-a-prius/

CEMEX. (2011). *Building a better future: 2010 sustainable development report.* Monterrey: CEMEX.

CEMEX, ITESM, World Bank. (2011). *Centro Virtual para la Innovacion y el Desarrollo Sustentable.* Retrieved February 12, 2012, from http://www.cca. org.mx/lideres/centrorse/unete/index.htm

Cengage. (2012). *Cengage learning: An overview,* Retrieved March 17, 2012, from http://www.cengage.com/about/

Chamberlain, G. (2011). *Revealed: True cost of the Christmas toys we buy from China's factories.* Retrieved March 6, 2012, from The Guardian: http://www. guardian.co.uk/world/2011/dec/04/chinese-toy-factories-christmas-disney

Cinépolis. (2008). *Del Amor nace la Vista.* Santa Fé: Cinépolis.

Clark, T. (2011). *Best sustainable apps for mobile devices.* Retrieved February 24, 2012, from ThomasNet News: http://news.thomasnet.com/green_clean/2011/10/20/best-sustainable-apps-for-mobile-devices/

Clark, E. (2002). *Trouble in Disneyland.* Retrieved March 6, 2012, from BBC News: http://news.bbc.co.uk/2/hi/business/2276093.stm

Clawson Freeo, S. K. (2011). *Crisis communication plan: A PR blue print.* Retrieved from http://www3.niu.edu/newsplace/crisis

Clorox Reporting. (2012). Retrieved March 24, 2012, from https://www. globalreporting.org/Pages/FR-Clorox-2011.aspx

CNN Money. (2011a). *World's most admired companies.* Retrieved March 6, 2012, from CNN Money: http://money.cnn.com/magazines/fortune/mostadmired/2011/best_worst/best4.html

CNN Money. (2011b). *The World's most admired companies.* Retrieved 30 March, 2012, from Best & worst in Social Responsibility: http://money.cnn.com/magazines/fortune/mostadmired/2011/best_worst/best4.html

CNN Money. (2011c). Retrieved March 6, 2012, from http://money.cnn.com/ magazines/fortune/global500/2011/snapshots/10460.html

The Coca Cola Company. (2011). *Introducing PlantBottle.* Retrieved February 12, 2012, from The Coca Cola Company: http://www.thecoca-colacompany. com/citizenship/plantbottle.html

Coca Cola Sustainability. (2012). Retrieved from http://www.thecoca-colacompany.com/sustainabilityreport/in-our-company/from-our-ceo.html

Coca Cola 2020 Vision. (2012). *Mission, vision & values,* Retrieved March 8, 2012, from http://www.thecoca-colacompany.com/ourcompany/mission_ vision_values.html

Confino, J. (2010). *Can you help us with our latest sustainability report?* Retrieved February 24, 2012, from Guardian News and Media: http://www.guardian. co.uk/sustainability/blog/sustainability-audit

Coombs, W. T. (2011). *The Handbook of crisis communication.* Hoboken, NJ: John Wiley & Sons, Inc.

Coombs, W. T. (2002). Assessing online issue threats: Issue contagions and their effect on issue prioritization. *Journal of Public Affairs 2(4)*, 215–229.

Danone. (2010). *Construyamos sus sueños Danone 2010.* Retrieved March 6, 2012, from Youtube: http://www.youtube.com/watch?v=FJts43pWr74

David, F. R. (1989). How companies define their mission. *Long Range Planning 22(1)*, 90–97.

David, F. R. (2007). *Strategic management: Concepts* (11 ed.). Upper Saddle River, NJ: Pearson.

Der Spiegel. (2008). *Deutsche Bank: Ackermann lehnt weiter jede Hilfe vom Staat ab [Ackermann].* Retrieved November 11, 2012, from Der Spiegel: http:// www.spiegel.de/wirtschaft/0,1518,587969,00.html

Development Crossing. (2012). Retrieved February 28, 2012, from Development Crossing: http://www.developmentcrossing.com/

Dow Jones Sustainability Index (DJSI). (2011). *Supersector leaders 2011.* Retrieved March 21, 2012, from http://www.sustainability-indexes.com/ review/supersector-leaders-2011.jsp

DJSI Brazil. (2011). *Sustainability leader: Member of DJSI world.* Retrieved March 21, 1012, from http://www.sustainability-indexes.com/images/supersector-leader-report-itausa_tcm1071-337446.pdf

DJSI Lotte. (2011). *Sustainability leader: Member of DJSI world, DJSI Asia Pacific, DJSI Korea.* Retrieved March 21, 1012, from http://www.sustainability-indexes.com/images/supersector-leader-report-lotte_tcm1071-337450.pdf

DJSI Westpac Banking. (2011). *Sustainability leader: Member of DJSI world, DJSI Asia Pacific.* Retrieved March 21, 1012, from http://www.sustainability-indexes.com/images/supersector-leader-report-westpac_tcm1071-337469.pdf

Du, S., Bhattacharya, C., & Sen, S. (2007). Reaping relational rewards from corporate social responsibility: The role of competitive positioning. *International Journal of Research in Marketing 24*(4), 224–241.

Earthimprints. (2011). *Biodegradable corn pen with seeds.* Retrieved March 6, 2012, from Earthimprints: http://www.earthimprints.com/writing-corn-seed-pens?size=_original

Economist Intelligence Unit. (2008). *Doing good: Business and the sustainability challenge.* London: The Economist.

Elkington, J. (1998). *Cannibals with forks: The triple bottom line of 21st century business.* Gabriola Island: New Society Publishers.

Eklund, K. (2012). Retrieved February 28, 2012, from World Without Oil: http://www.worldwithoutoil.org/metacontact.htm

Emsden, C. (February 29, 2012). Luxottica upbeat for 2012. *The Wall Street Journal.* Retrieved December 29, 2012, from www.wsj.com

Environmental Leader. (2008). *Chevron 'A+,' Google 'F' in sustainability reporting efforts.* Retrieved February 23, 2012, from Environmental Leader: http://www.environmentalleader.com/2008/06/19/chevron-a-google-f-in-sustainability-reporting-efforts/

Ethics Resource Center. (2011). Retrieved from http://www.ethics.org/resource/accepting-responsibility-responsibly-corporate-response-times-crisis

Ethics Resource Center. (2012). *Ethics glossary.* Retrieved December 9, 2011, from http://www.ethics.org/resource/ethics-glossary

Ethical Trading Initiative. (2012). *Respect for workers worldwide.* Retrieved March 23, 2012, from http://www.ethicaltrade.org/eti-base-code

Fairtrade Monitoring. (2011). *Monitoring the scope and benefits of Fairtrade* (3rd ed.). Retrieved from http://www.fairtrade.net/fileadmin/user_upload/content/2009/resources/Monitoring_the_scope_and_benefits_of_Fairtrade_2011.pdf

Fernando, R., & Purkayasth, D. (2007). *The body shop: Social resonsibility or sustained greenwashing.* Retrieved June 26, 2011, from OIKOS: http://www.oikos-international.org/en/academic/case-collection/inspection-copies/alphabetical-list.html

Fields, M. (2009). *Enough with the princesses!* Retrieved March 6, 2012, from The Root: http://www.theroot.com/views/enough-princesses

The Food & Drink Innovation Network. (2011). *Ben & Jerry's launches new fairtrade ice cream.* Retrieved March 6, 2012, from The Food & Drink Innovation Network: http://www.fdin.org.uk/2011/03/ben-jerrys-launches-new-fairtrade-ice-cream/

Forbes. (2011). Retrieved December 29, 2011, from http://www.forbes.com/sites/eco-nomics/2011/10/18/newsweek-names-ibm-greenest-company-in-america/

Foresight Sustainable Business Alliance. (2012). *Anti-greenwashing code of ethics*. Retrieved December 19, 2011, from http://www.foresightdesign.org/business/code-of-ethics.php

Freeman, E. (1984). *Strategic management: A stakeholder approach*. New York: Free Press.

Freeman, R. E. (2010). *Strategic management: A stakeholder approach*. Cambridge: Cambridge University Press.

Fuchs, C. (2008). The implications of new information and communication technologies for sustainability. *Environment, Development and Sustainability 10*(3), 291–309.

The Fun Theory. (2012). Retrieved from http://thefuntheory.com/

General Electric. (2012). *Ecomagination*. Retrieved February 24, 2012, from Twitter: http://twitter.com/#!/ecomagination/statuses/38681227045249024

Given, K. (2011). *Social entrepreneur funding series: Crowdfunding your startup*. Retrieved February 28, 2012, from Green Marketing: http://www.greenmarketing.tv/2011/03/16/social-entrepreneur-funding-options-crowdfunding/

Glaxosmithkline. (2012). *Corporate responsibility report 2010*. Retrieved March 10, 2012, from http://www.gsk.com/responsibility/downloads/GSK-CR-2010-Report.pdf

Global Reporting Initiative. (2012). *Information*. Retrieved March 24, 2012, from https://www.globalreporting.org/information/about-gri/what-is-GRI/Pages/default.aspx

Global Reporting Initiative. (2012a). *Reference sheet*. Retrieved March 23, 2012, from https://www.globalreporting.org/resourcelibrary/G3.1-Quick-Reference-Sheet.pdf

Global Reporting Initiative. (2012b). *Sustainability reporting guidelines*. Retrieved March 23, 2012, from https://www.globalreporting.org/resourcelibrary/G3.1-Sustainability-Reporting-Guidelines.pdf

Google. (2012). *Google company*. Retrieved February 23, 2012, from http://www.google.com/about/company/

Greenberg, J. & Elliott, C. (2009). A cold cut crisis: Listeriosis, maple leaf foods, and the politics of apology. *Canadian Journal of Communication 34*(2), 189–204.

Greenbiz.com. (2010). *Starbucks tackles green goals except one: Recycling*. Retrieved from http://www.greenbiz.com/news/2010/04/19/starbucks-tackles-green-goals-except-one-recycling

Greenbiz.com. (2012). *Green and sustainable marketing, communications, and reporting*. Retrieved March 30, 2012, from http://www.greenbiz.com/section/marketing-communications

Greenpeace. (2010). *Recapping on BP's long history of greenwashing*. Retrieved October 15, 2011, from Greenpeace, USA: http://www.greenpeace.org/

usa/en/news-and-blogs/campaign-blog/recapping-on-bps-long-history-of-greenwashing/blog/26025/

Greenwald, R. (Director). (2005). *The high cost of low price* [Motion Picture].

Greenwood, J. (2011). When sorry is not enough: The steps to brand redemption are steep, but ultimately worth the effort. *The Wall Street Journal.* Retrieved October 18, 2011, from www.wsj.com

Guardian. (2012a). *Twitter users not lovin' McDonald's.* Retrieved February 28, 2012, from Mediamonkey: http://www.guardian.co.uk/media/mediamonkeyblog/2012/jan/25/twitter-mcdonalds-good-news-stories

Guardian. (2012b). *WikiLeaks.* Retrieved March 1, 2012, from Guardian: http://www.guardian.co.uk/media/wikileaks

Gunther, M. (2011). *How McDonald's is mainstreaming sustainability.* Retrieved December 29, 2011 from http://www.greenbiz.com/blog/2011/12/21/how-mcdonalds-mainstreaming-sustainability

Halbright, R., & Dunn, M. (2010). Case study: The Toyota Prius. *Managerial Marketing.* Retrieved from http://www.maxdunn.com/files/attachments/maxdunn/PMBA:%20Presidio%20MBA%20Home/Prius_Marketing_Case_Study.pdf

Hasbro. (2012). *Trouble disney pixar cars 2 edition game.* Retrieved March 6, 2012, from Hasbro Games: http://www.hasbro.com/games/en_US/shop/details.cfm?R=8E210857-5056-900B-10C1-7FA9AE8FE6FD:en_US

Hendler, J. (2009). Web 3.0 emerging. *Compute 42*(1), 88–90.

Hitt, M. A., Ireland, R. D., & Hoskisson, R. E. (2011). *Strategic management: Competitiveness and globalization, concepts and cases* (9th ed.). Mason, OH: Cengage/South-Western Publishers.

Horiuchi, R., Schuchard, R., Shea, L., & Townsend, S. (2009). *Understanding and preventing greenwash: A business guide.* San Francisco, CA: BSR.

Howe, J. (2006). The rise of crowdsourcing. *Computer and Information Science 14*(14), 1–5.

Icebreaker. (2012). *Baacode.* Retrieved February 24, 2012, from Icebreaker: http://baacode.icebreaker.com/site/baacode/index.html

Iezzi, T. (November 3, 2008,). J&J's green-packaging rebirth proves power of smart design. *Advertising Age* (Chicago) *79*(41), 16.

Innocent. (2012a). *Our approach to being sustainable.* London: Innocent.

Innocent. (2012b). *Innocent.* Retrieved February 18, 2012, from http://www.innocentdrinks.co.uk/us/press/about-innocent#/us/press/about-innocent

Innocent Kids. (2012). *Innocent smoothies for kids.* Retrieved February 18, 2012, rom http://www.innocentkids.co.uk/

Institute for Crisis Management. (2011). *Accepting responsibility responsibly: Corporate response in times of crisis.* Retrieved December 13, 2011 from http://www.crisisexperts.com/crisisdef_main.htm

Itaúsa. (2010). *Annual sustainability report*. Retrieved March 24, 2012, from http://ww13.itau.com.br/itausa/HTML/en-US/infofinan/rao.htm#

Itaúsa. (2012). *Information*. Retrieved March 24, 2012, from http://ww13.itau.com.br/itausa/HTML/en-US/infofinan/dcc/quemsomos.htm

Jack, W., & Suri, T. (2010). *The economics of M-PESA*. Retrieved February 24, 2012, from Massachusetts Institute of Technology: http://www.mit.edu/~tavneet/M-PESA.pdf

Jargon, J. (May 18, 2011). McDonald's under pressure to fire Ronald. *The Wall Street Journal*. Retrieved from www.wsj.com

Keefe, B. (2008). *Meet Google's chief sustainability officer (What a cool job!)*. Retrieved February 23, 2012, from Divine Caroline: http://www.divinecaroline.com/22277/44799-meet-google-s-chief-sustainability-officer/

Keene, A. (2007). *'Email a duck, raise a buck' by Munchkin for Susan G. Komen*. Retrieved March 1, 2012, from Cause Marketing: http://causerelatedmarketing.blogspot.com/2007/10/email-duck-raise-buck-by-munchkin-for.html

Knapp, M., & Hall, J. (2010). *Nonverbal communication* (7th ed.). Boston, MA: Wadsworth.

Koehler, D. A. & Park, C. (2011). How companies are making eco-labels core to sustainability strategy. Retrieved February 18, 2012, from http://www.greenbiz.com/blog/2011/11/15/how-companies-are-making-eco-labels-core-sustainability-strategy

Kotler, P., Kartajaya, H., & Setiawan, I. (2010). *Marketing 3.0: from products to customers to the human spirit*. Hoboken, NJ: Wiley.

Kotler, P., & Lee, N. (2004). *Corporate social responsibility: Doing the most good for your company and your cause*. Chichester: Wiley.

Kron, J. (2008). *The importance of being Google's sustainability report*. Retrieved February 23, 2012, from Trillium Asset Management: http://trilliuminvest.com/news-articles-category/advocacy-news-articles/the-importance-of-being-google%E2%80%99s-sustainability-report/

Laasch, O., & Conaway, R. (2011). "Making it do" at the movies theatres: Communicating sustainability at the workplace. *Business Communication Quarterly 74*(1), 68–78.

Laasch, O., & Conaway, R. N. (2012). *Responsible business: From management theory to real-life change*. Monterrey: Editorial Digital ITESM.

Laasch, O., & Flores, U. (2010). Implementing profitable CSR: The CSR 2.0 business compass. In M. Pohl, & N. Tolhurst (Eds.), *Responsible business: How to manage a CSR strategy successfully* (pp. 289–309). Chichester: John Wiley & Sons Ltd.

Lane, R. (2011). *The United Nations says broadband is basic human right*. Retrieved February 16, 2012, from Forbes: http://www.forbes.com/sites/

randalllane/2011/11/15/the-united-nations-says-broadband-is-basic-human-right/

Larsen & Toubro Company. (2012). Retrieved March 20, 2012 from https://www.globalreporting.org/Pages/FR-Larsen-and-Toubro-2012.aspx

Lassila, O., & Hendler, J. (2007). Embracing "Web 3.0". *IEEE Internet Computing 11*(3), 90–93.

LEGO. (2011). *Criticism of LEGO licensed products manufactured in China.* Retrieved March 6, 2012, from LEGO: http://aboutus.lego.com/en-us/newsroom/2011/december/criticism-of-lego-licensed-products-manufactured-in-china/

LEGO. (2012a). *Does the LEGO group condone war toys?* Retrieved March 6, 2012, from LEGO Answers: http://bricks.stackexchange.com/questions/291/does-the-lego-group-condone-war-toys

LEGO. (2012b). *LEGO ambassadors 2012.* Retrieved March 6, 2012, from LEGO: http://aboutus.lego.com/en-gb/lego-group/programs-and-visits/lego-ambassador/

LEGO. (2012c). *The whole child product timeline.* Retrieved March 6, 2012, from LEGO: http://parents.lego.com/en-us/Default.aspx

LEGO Group. (2010). *Progress report.* Billund: Corporate Governance & Sustainability and Corporate Communications.

Leipziger, D. (2010). *The corporate responsibility codebook.* Sheffield: Greenleaf.

Leopoldo, I. (2011). *Digital life: Today and tomorrow.* Retrieved February 16, 2012, from http://www.youtube.com/watch?v=iG8KaWxr2gs

Lesikar, R., & Petit, J. (1989). *Business communication: Theory and practice.* Homewood, IL: Richard D. Irwin, Inc.

Lewis, L. K. (2000). Communicating change: Four cases of quality programs. *The Journal of Business Communication, 37*(2), 128–155.

The Local. (2009). *Joschka Fischer working with BMW.* Retrieved February 12, 2012, from The Local: http://www.thelocal.de/money/20090920-22035.html

LOHAS. (2012). Retrieved February 24, 2012 from http://www.lohas.com/

Lopez, E., & Martinez, L. (2012). Redes sociales y responsabilidad social [Social networks and social responsibility]. *Taller las redes sociales y la RSE [Workshop social networks and CSR].* Mexico City: EXPOK.

Lotte Annual Report. (2010). Retrieved March 17, 2012 from http://www.lotteshoppingir.com/eng/data/data_02.jsp

Lotte Sustainability Report. (2011). Retrieved March 17, 2012 from http://unglobalcompact.org/system/attachments/12205/original/2011_Lotte_Shopping_Sustainability_Report_20110930.pdf?1317703908

Lovell, J. (December 9, 2007). Left-hand-turn elimination. *The New York Times Magazine.* Retrieved from http://www.nytimes.com/2007/12/09/magazine/09left-handturn.html

Lozanova, S. (June 10, 2009). *Starbucks coffee: Green or greenwashed?* Retrieved December 29, 2011, http://www.greenbiz.com/blog/2009/06/10/starbucks-coffee-green-or-greenwashed

Lundquist. (2010). *Lundquist CSR online awards 'Global Leaders' 2010: Assessing online CSR communications based on stakeholders' needs.* Milan: Lundquist.

Lutts, R. H. (1992). The trouble with Bambi: Walt Disney's Bambi and the American vision of nature. *Forest and Conservation History 36*(4), 160–171.

Makower, J. (September 9, 2010,). *Behind procter & Gamble's sustainability vision, Greenbiz.com.* Retrieved from http://www.greenbiz.com/blog/2010/09/27/behind-procter-gambles-sustainability-vision

Margolis, J., & Gomes Casseres, M. (2012). *The 10 best practices for sustainability reporting, Greenbiz.com.* Retrieved March 2, ,2012 from http://www.greenbiz.com/blog/2012/03/02/10-best-practices-sustainability-reporting?page=0%2C1

Massey, P. (2011). *The rise of crowdsourcing in corporate social responsibility.* Retrieved February 28, 2012, from The Huffington Post: http://www.huffingtonpost.com/paul-massey/the-rise-of-crowdsourcing_b_821357.html

Michael Baldinger, CEO, SAM. (2012). Retrieved from http://www.sustainability-index.com/djsi_pdf/news/PressReleases/110908-djsi-review-2011-e-vdef.pdf

Mitchel, R. K., Agle, B. R., & Wood, D. J. (1997). Toward a theory of stakeholder salience: Defining the principles of who and what really counts. *Academy of Management Review 22*(4), 853–886.

Morsing, M., & Schultz, M. (2006). Corporate social responsibility communication: stakeholder information, response and involvement strategies. *Business Ethics: A European Review 15*(4), 323–338.

Munich Airport Reporting. (2012). Retrieved March 17, 2012 from https://www.globalreporting.org/Pages/FR-Munich-Airport-2011.aspx

Net Impact. (2011). *Upcoming webinars.* Retrieved February 28, 2012, from Net Impact: http://netimpact.org/learn/

Newman's Own. (2012). Retrieved from http://newmansown.com/

Nielsen, J. (2006). *Participation inequality: Encouraging more users to contribute.* Retrieved February 28, 2012, from Useit: http://www.useit.com/alertbox/participation_inequality.html

Nike Code of Conduct. (2012). Retrieved from http://nikeinc.com/search?search_terms=code+of+conduct

Nijhof, A., Cludts, S., Fisscher, O., & Laan, A. (2003). Measuring the implementation of codes of conduct: An assessment method based on a process approach of the responsible organization. *Journal of Business Ethics 45*(1–2), 65–78.

Obama, B. (2012). *Transparency and open government.* Retrieved February 22, 2012, from http://www.whitehouse.gov/the_press_office/TransparencyandOpenGovernment

OneSight Foundation. (2011). Retrieved December 12, 2011 from www.onesight.org

O'Reilly, T. (2005). *What is Web 2.0: Design patterns and business models for the next generation of software.* Retrieved August 30, 2011, from O'Reilley Network: http://www.oreillynet.com/lpt/a/6228

Palazzo, B. (2010). An introduction to stakeholder dialogue. In M. Pohl, & N. Tolhurst (Eds.), *Responsible business: How to manage a CSR strategy successfully* (pp. 17–42). Chichester, West Sussex, UK: John Wiley & Sons Ltd.

Palmquist, R. (2010). *Student campaign takes on Nike like never before.* Retrieved February 11, 2012, from Huff Post: http://www.huffingtonpost.com/rod-palmquist/student-campaign-takes-on_b_643375.html

Pariser, E. (2011). *The filter bubble: What the Internet is hiding from you.* London: Penguin Books.

Pearce, J. A., & David, F. (1987). Corporate mission statements: The bottom line. *Academy of Management Executive 1*(2), 109–116.

PepsiCo. (2012). Retrieved February 28, 2012, from Pepsi Refresh Project: http://www.refresheverything.com/index

PepsiCo Vision. (2012). Retrieved from http://www.pepsico.com/Company/Our-Mission-and-Vision.html

Peters, A. (2011). *Using gamification to make the world a better place.* Retrieved October 12, 2011, from GreenBiz.com: http://www.greenbiz.com/blog/2011/07/03/using-gamification-make-world-better-place?page=0%2C2

Porter, M. (1985). *Competitive advantage: Creating and sustaining superior performance.* New York: The Free Press.

Prahalad, C. K. (2010). *The fortune at the bottom of the pyramid: Eradicating poverty through profits* (5th anniversary ed.). Upper Saddle River, NJ: Pearson.

Preuss, L. (2010). Codes of conduct in organisational context: From cascade to lattice-work of codes. *Journal of Business Ethics 94*(4), 471–487.

Procter & Gamble. (2008). Retrieved from http://www.pg.com/en_US/downloads/sustainability/reports/PG_2008_Sustainability_Report.pdf

Proctor and Gamble Annual Report. (2011). Retrieved March 14, 2012 from http://annualreport.pg.com/annualreport2011/sustainability/

Procter & Gamble. (2011a). *Little actions big difference.* Retrieved February 24, 2012, from Future Friendly: http://www.futurefriendly.co.uk/home.aspx

Procter & Gamble. (2011b). *Helping consumers conserve.* Retrieved February 24, 2012, from P&G: http://www.pg.com/en_US/sustainability/environmental_sustainability/products_packaging/consumer_education.shtml

Proctor and Gamble Mission Statement. (2005). Retrieved March 14, 2012 from http://www.pg.com/en_US/company/purpose_people/index.shtml

Proctor and Gamble, Purpose-values-principles statement. (2011). Retrieved March 14, 2012 from http://www.pg.com/translations/pvp_pdf/english_PVP.pdf

PUMA. (2012). Retrieved from http://about.puma.com/category/company/glance/

Raftery, T. (2010). *Tech company sustainability reports reviewed—updated.* Retrieved February 23, 2012, from GreenMonk: the blog: http://greenmonk.net/tech-company-sustainability-reports-reviewed/

Regenwald. (2012). Retrieved March 1, 2012, from Regenwald: http://www.regenwald.org/

Rogers, P., Gunesekera, M., & Yang, M.L. (2011). Language options for managing: Dana Corporation's philosophy and policy document. *Journal of Business Communication 48(3)*, 256–299.

Samsung. (2012). *Global harmony with people, society & environment: 2011 sustainability report.* Suwon: Samsung Electronics.

Savage, G. T., Nix, T. W., Whitehead, C. J., & Blair, J. D. (1991). Strategies for assessing and managing organizational stakeholders. *Academy of Management Executive 5, 2*(5), 61–75.

Schwienbacher, A., & Larralde, B. (2010). Crowdfunding of small entrepreneurial ventures. In D. Cumming (Ed.), *The Oxford handbook of entreprenurial finance* (pp. 369–391). New York: Oxford University Press.

Seelos, C. & Mair, J. (2004). *The Sekem initiative,* case study obtained through Harvard Business Publishing for Educators. Retrieved from http://cb.hbsp.harvard.edu

SEKEM. (2012). Retrieved from http://www.sekem.com/

Sherman, E., Moore, M. M., Creamer, M., Rooney, J., et al. (2006, October 2). 10 of the best in the business. *Advertising Age* (Chicago) *77*(40), 13.

The SIGMA Project. (2012). *SIGMA project guidelines.* Retrieved from http://www.projectsigma.co.uk/Guidelines/default.asp

Smart, J. (2007). *Metaverse roadmap.* Retrieved February 24, 2012, from http://metaverseroadmap.org/inputs4.html#glossary

Sobczak, A. (2006). Are codes of conduct in global supply chains really voluntary? From soft law regulations of labour regulations to consumer law. *Business Ethics Quarterly 16*(2), 167–184.

Social Mention. (2012). *Frequently asked questions.* Retrieved February 24, 2012, from Social Mention: http://www.socialmention.com/faq#1

Sourcemap. (2012). *TOMS.* Retrieved February 24, 2012, from Sourcemap: http://sourcemap.com/view/1438

Starbucks Global Responsibility Report: Goals and Progress. (2010). Retrieved from http://www.starbucks.com/responsibility/learn-more/goals-and-progress/recycling

Strauss, L. (2010). *What's the future of line drying?* Retrieved February 24, 2012, from Levi Strauss & Co.: http://www.levistrauss.com/news/press-releases/levi-strauss-co-asks-what-s-future-line-drying

Story, L. (2008). *Can burt's bees turn clorox green?* Retrieved May 28, 2011, from New York Times: http://www.nytimes.com/2008/01/06/business/06bees.html?pagewanted=1

Sullivan, M. (2006). *Crowdfunding.* Retrieved February 28, 2012, from The Crowdfunding Wiki: http://crowdfunding.pbworks.com/w/page/10402176/Crowdfunding

SustainAbility. (2008). *The social intrapreneur: A field guide for corporate change makers.* London: SustainAbility.

SustainAbility. (2011). *Survey on sustainable consumption.* London: SustainAbility.

Taubken, N., & Leibold, I. (2010). Ten rules for succesful CSR communication. In M. Pohl, & N. Tolhurst (Eds.), *Responsible business: How to manage a CSR strategy successfully* (pp. 129–142). Chichester, West Sussex, UK: John Wiley & Sons Ltd.

Taylor, A. (2006). *Toyota: The birth of the prius.* Retrieved June 12, 2011, from CNN money: http://money.cnn.com/2006/02/17/news/companies/mostadmired_fortune_toyota/index.htm

Thoma, K. (2011). *Re-opening ceremony of the Deutsche Bank towers.* Retrieved February 12, 2012, from Deutsche Bank: http://www.db.com/medien/en/content/press_releases_2011_3536.htm

Thorson, E., & Moore, J. (1996). *Integrated communication.* Mahwah: Lawrence Erlbaum Associates.

Timberland. (2011). *Report builder.* Retrieved February 23, 2012, from Timberland Responsibility: http://responsibility.timberland.com/reporting/report-builder/

Timberland. (2012a). *Home: Social networks.* Retrieved February 23, 2012, from Timberland: http://community.timberland.com/Social-Networks

Timberland. (2012b). *Timberland Hortiscope.* Retrieved February 23, 2012, from Facebook: http://www.facebook.com/timberland?sk=info

Timberland. (2012c). *Earthkeepers.* Retrieved February 23, 2012, from Timberland: http://earthkeepers.timberland.com/#/home

Timberland. (2012d). *The bootmakers blog.* Retrieved February 23, 2012, from Timberland: http://blog.timberland.com/

Timberland. (2012e). *@Timberland.* Retrieved February 24, 2012, from Twitter: http://twitter.com/#!/Timberland

Timberland. (2012f). *Timberland earthkeepers: Virtual forest.* Retrieved February 24, 2012, from Facebook: http://apps.facebook.com/timberlandtreeapp/; http://community.timberland.com/Haiti

TOMS. (2011). *Giving report..* (http://www.toms.com/giving-report)

TOMS. (2012). *TOMS.* Retrieved February 11, 2012, from http://www.toms.com/

TOMS Shoes. (2009). *TOMS: A history.* Retrieved September 5, 2011, from Youtube: http://www.youtube.com/watch?v=PTQsQUu1Ho8

TOMS Shoes. (2012a). Retrieved from http://www.toms.com/

TOMS Shoes. (2012b). *One million thank yous*. Retrieved March 6, 2012, from TOMS: http://www.toms.com/onemillion

Torry, H., & Sherr, I. (March 2, 2012). German Court dismisses Samsung, Apple patent suits. *The Wall Street Journal*. Retrieved from www.wsj.com

Toyota Global Vision. (2012). Retrieved March 14, 2012 from http://www.toyota-global.com/company/vision_philosophy/toyota_global_vision_2020.html

Toyota US Vision. (2012). Retrieved March 14, 2012 from http://www.toyota.com/help/faqs/company-what_are_toyotas_mission_and_vision_statements.html

Twain, M. (n.d.). *Mark Twain quotes*. Retrieved March 1, 2012, from BrainyQuote: http://www.brainyquote.com/quotes/quotes/m/marktwain162937.html#ixzz1nJaKuri

United Airlines. (2012). Retrieved from http://pss.united.com/web/en-US/content/company/globalcitizenship/environment_faq.aspx#4

United Nations Environment Programme. (2006). *Sustainability communications: A toolkit for marketing and advertising courses*. Nairobi: UNEP.

United Nations Global Compact. (2011). Retrieved from http://unglobalcompact.org/participants/detail/6197-Lotte-Shopping-Co-Ltd

United Parcel Service [UPS]. (2012). Retrieved from http://www.ups.com/content/us/en/about/facts/worldwide.html

Varadarajan, P. R., & Menon, A. (1988). Cause-related marketing: A coalignment of marketing strategy and corporate philanthropy. *Journal of Marketing 52*(3), 58–74.

Waller, R. L., & Conaway, R. N. (2011). Framing and counterframing the issue of corporate social responsibility: The communication strategies of Nikebiz.com. *Journal of Business Communication 48*(1), 83–106.

Walmart. (2010). *Standards for suppliers*. Retrieved May 9, 2011, from Ethical Sourcing: http://walmartstores.com/AboutUs/279.aspx

Walmart Annual Report. (2011). Retrieved from http://walmartstores.com/sites/AnnualReport/2011/mission.aspx (there is neither author, nor publisher for those reports) Walmart Sustainability. (2012). Retrieved from http://walmartstores.com/Sustainability/

Weaver, R. M. (1948). *Ideas have consequences*. Chicago, IL: University of Chicago Press.

Webster, D. (2011). *IP traffic to quadruple by 2015*. Retrieved February 16, 2012, from Cisco: http://blogs.cisco.com/sp/ip-traffic-to-quadruple-by-2015/

Weinreich, N. K. (2011). *Hands-on social marketing: A step-by-step guide to designing change for good* (2nd ed.). Thousand Oaks, CA: SAGE Publications.

Westpac Bank. (2012). Retrieved from http://www.westpac.com.au/about-westpac/the-westpac-group/company-overview/our-strategy-vision/

White, G. B. (2009). *Sustainability reporting: Managing for wealth and corporate health.* New York: Business Expert Press, LLC.

Williams, L. S. (2008). The mission statement: A corporate reporting tool with a past, present, and future. *Journal of Business Communication 45(*2), 94–119.

York, E. B. (June 8, 2009,). *Advertising age* (Midwest region Ed.), *80(21)*, 12.

Yunus, M. (2010). *Building social business: The new kind of capitalism that serves humanity's most pressing needs.* New York: PublicAffairs.

Zweifel, D. (2001). *Truth voids Nike's free speech offer.* Retrieved March 1, 2012, from Common Dreams: www.commondreams.org/views01/0320-06.htm

Index

Announcing the Business Expert Press Digital Library

Concise E-books Business Students Need for Classroom and Research

This book can also be purchased in an e-book collection by your library as

- a one-time purchase,
- that is owned forever,
- allows for simultaneous readers,
- has no restrictions on printing, and
- can be downloaded as PDFs from within the library community.

Our digital library collections are a great solution to beat the rising cost of textbooks. e-books can be loaded into their course management systems or onto student's e-book readers.

The **Business Expert Press** digital libraries are very affordable, with no obligation to buy in future years. For more information, please visit **www.businessexpertpress.com/librarians**. To set up a trial in the United States, please contact **Adam Chesler** at *adam.chesler@businessexpertpress. com* for all other regions, contact **Nicole Lee** at *nicole.lee@igroupnet.com*.

OTHER TITLES IN OUR CORPORATE COMMUNICATION COLLECTION

Collection Editors: **Debbie DuFrene and Stephen F. Austin**

- *Managing Investor Relations: Strategies for Effective Communication* by Alexander Laskin
- *Managing Virtual Teams* by Debbie DuFrene
- *Corporate Communication: Tactical Guidelines for Strategic Practice* by Michael Goodman, Peter B. Hirsch
- *Communication Strategies for Today's Managerial Leader* by Deborah Roebuck
- *Fundamentals of Writing for Marketing and Public Relations: A Step-by-Step Guide for Quick and Effective Results* by Janet Mizrahi

www.ingramcontent.com/pod-product-compliance
Lightning Source LLC
Chambersburg PA
CBHW060544210326
41519CB00014B/3335